Praise for

The SACRED ANDEAN CODES

"Long before the birth of modern science, the secrets of life were revealed and preserved for future generations among a clan of wisdomkeepers hidden high in the mountains of the Peruvian Andes. Marcela Lobos reveals these ancient secrets and more in her book The Sacred Andean Codes. In an intimate sharing of her apprenticeship with the descendants of that clan—the Q'uero people of today—Lobos reveals how the direct experience of the Munay-Ki initiations can shape our perception of life's challenges, while leading us into our deepest healing and highest dreams. Whether you're an artist or an engineer, a homemaker or policy maker, this book is about you, your life, and every relationship that you'll ever experience. Lobos' compelling truths of earth wisdom linger in our hearts long after we read the pages of The Sacred Andean Codes, reminding us that we're always more than the challenges that life brings to our doorstep."

— **Gregg Braden**, *New York Times* best-selling author of
The God Code and *The Divine Matrix*

"The Sacred Andean Codes *is a magnificent book. Marcela Lobos gives us a comprehensive understanding of the Munay-Ki initiations. The wisdom of these 10 initiations will connect you with your authentic self and root you in the flow of life. Marcela is the perfect person to transmit these powerful rites to us. She writes and teaches in a masterful way while bringing in deep feminine wisdom. You will learn how to reach your highest spiritual potential—this is a true gift Marcela shares with us in this beautiful book."*

— **Sandra Ingerman**, international shamanic teacher and award-winning
author of 12 books, including *Soul Retrieval: Mending the
Fragmented Self* and *The Book of Ceremony*

"Most current books about creating a better life focus on speed: life hacks, shortcuts, and mechanistic systems. But true transformation lies beyond such strategies. In The Sacred Andean Codes, Marcela Lobos encourages us to find our inherent wisdom by slowing down. She writes lovingly and clearly about the Munay-Ki (10 shamanic initiations) as a time-honored way to connect with and empower your true self. Her work will help you go beyond self-help to encounter true spiritual awakening."

— **Susan Piver**, *New York Times* best-selling author of *The Buddhist Enneagram*

The
SACRED
ANDEAN
CODES

The

SACRED
ANDEAN
CODES

10 SHAMANIC INITIATIONS
*to Heal Past Wounds, Awaken Your Conscious
Evolution, and Reveal Your Destiny*

MARCELA LOBOS

HAY HOUSE

Carlsbad, California • New York City
London • Sydney • New Delhi

Published in the United Kingdom by:
Hay House UK Ltd, The Sixth Floor, Watson House,
54 Baker Street, London W1U 7BU
Tel: +44 (0)20 3927 7290; Fax: +44 (0)20 3927 7291; www.hayhouse.co.uk

Published in the United States of America by:
Hay House Inc., PO Box 5100, Carlsbad, CA 92018-5100
Tel: (1) 760 431 7695 or (800) 654 5126
Fax: (1) 760 431 6948 or (800) 650 5115; www.hayhouse.com

Published in Australia by:
Hay House Australia Ltd, 18/36 Ralph St, Alexandria NSW 2015
Tel: (61) 2 9669 4299; Fax: (61) 2 9669 4144; www.hayhouse.com.au

Published in India by:
Hay House Publishers India, Muskaan Complex, Plot No.3, B-2,
Vasant Kunj, New Delhi 110 070
Tel: (91) 11 4176 1620; Fax: (91) 11 4176 1630; www.hayhouse.co.in

A catalogue record for this book is available from the British Library.

Tradepaper ISBN: 978-1-78817-941-6
E-book ISBN: 978-1-4019-7289-9
Audiobook ISBN: 978-1-4019-7290-5

Printed and bound by CPI Group (UK) Ltd, Croydon, CR0 4YY

To my granddaughter Lina
and to all the children of the world

CONTENTS

FOREWORD

by Alberto Villoldo, Ph.D.

Mystical origin stories are envisioned as multi-dimensional spirals rather than linear tales—especially when referencing "new" rites of passage. Paradoxically, I feel drawn to begin this Foreword with a chronological description of how I first encountered the destiny-altering initiations known as the Munay-Ki. May these words help you form a clear map for your journey with the rites.

In the early 1970s, I received a research grant to study the medicinal plants and healing practices of the Amazonian shamans. At the time, although I was fresh out of graduate school, I was directing a small research laboratory at San Francisco State University, studying if we could create not only psychosomatic disease but also health.

I was guided to this work by my professor, Dr. Stanley Krippner, with whom I had co-authored a book, *The Realms of Healing*. Dr. Krippner encouraged me to learn about the psychedelic plants that allow the shamans to glimpse the invisible world and about the powerful shrubs and barks that regenerate the body and the brain. While working with the shamans in the rainforest, I heard about the ancient mystery schools that had once thrived in the Andes and were destroyed by the Inquisition. I thought this was the stuff of legend until a renowned shaman from the city of Pucallpa—the last navigable port of the Amazon—said to me, "We can speak with the plants, and they heal and teach us. But the Andes is where the master shamans are."

I was intrigued. And then, in early 1972, during an ayahuasca ceremony in the Amazon, I had a vision of what appeared to be a city of gold. *Ahh,* I thought, *the legendary El Dorado that so many explorers had searched for.* A week later I boarded a flight to Lima, the capital of Peru, and then embarked on a seven-day bus ride to Cusco, the seat of the ancient Inka Empire, to see if I could meet one of these master shamans and find anyone who knew of the City of Gold.

In Cusco, later that fall, I learned that Machu Picchu was known as the City of Light. In this visit I met and befriended Dr. Manuel Chávez Ballón, then chief archaeologist in Machu Picchu. He spoke to me about a city known as "Choquequirao" (the City of Gold) that few had explored. We promptly set about planning an expedition to the archaeological site. My sponsors from the United States were happy to fund this adventure. But Peru at that time was overrun by Maoist guerrillas, and we were never able to make it—Marcela would be the one to explore the fabled City of Gold in 2009 and then hike beyond it to Vilcabamba (the Sacred Place), and then go on to Espiritu Pampa (the Place of the Spirits). These were the four sacred cities of the Inka, each one farther from the physical world of people and closer to the invisible spirit world. To this date very few people have explored the four fabled "secret cities" of the Inka. I am convinced that these are the real El Dorado, not walls covered in gold, but the real treasure of the Inka: the Secret Knowledge.

During my first visit to Cusco, Dr. Cháves Ballón told me about an expedition he had led to the Q'ero communities, the last descendants of the Inka. The Q'ero had remained invisible to the West for 500 years, living in villages above 15,000 feet, where the Spanish conquerors never found them. They spoke a perfect Quechua and maintained their ancient customs. The members of that original expedition to the Q'ero included the archaeologist Óscar Núñez del Prado, whose son, Juan, would later become a prominent teacher of the Andean traditions and a personal friend.

In the early 1970s, Dr. Cháves Ballón's home in Cuzco was a buzzing mecca of Indigenous students from the University of Cusco. They were helping him paint murals reproducing the ceremonial art of the Inka. He had a passion for the iconography of the ancient peoples of the Andes, the imagery found in the weavings and ceramics. Local farmers would bring him pottery they had uncovered while tilling the soil, as they knew they would receive a meal and a reward from the good doctor, who would copy the art and then turn over the valued ceramics to the archaeological museum.

Dr. Cháves Ballón would be my academic mentor for the next three decades until his death. At his home I would meet the first Q'ero villagers. I remember my initial contact with the Q'ero and how it made me most uncomfortable. Whereas Andean Indians looked down at the ground when you spoke with them (a submissive gesture taught to their ancestors by the conquistadors, who insisted that anyone of European descent be addressed as *wiracocha*, or "god"), the Q'ero looked you in the eyes, unflinching. They seemed to gaze into your soul, to discover who you were inside. At Dr. Cháves Ballón's studio, the Q'ero would wear their colorful red ponchos woven with the royal seal of the Inka—they were the only Andeans permitted to have the royal emblem in their attire. Yet, when they left the studio, they would don vanilla-colored ponchos with no markings on them. Otherwise, people would stone them, for the Church had spread rumors that these men and women were "witches." On one occasion, I saw a mother run up to the *paqos*, with her baby in her arms, asking them to bless her child.

It was not until 1982, with my friend Américo Yabar, that I met the high paqos (or most respected shamans). Américo's family had been the heirs to a Spanish land grant that included the Q'ero villages. At the once-grand family hacienda known as Mullu Marka, I met Don Manuel Quispe. He was the eldest *Alto Mesayok*, or Wisdomkeeper, and the one who would initiate me into the lineage of Andean sages.

Don Manuel accompanied me on numerous expeditions through the Andes. One day in the spring of 1995, he asked me to invite my top students to join the shamans on a pilgrimage to Mount Ausangate. The following year, 20 of my students and I hiked and rode horses to our base camp by the Blue Lagoon. We had come prepared to host and feed 5 or 10 paqos. The following day, Don Manuel appeared with nearly 100 Q'ero men, women, and children who had walked for three days from their mountain villages to join us. We were to help them bring in a new *karpay,* the Mosoq or New Rite.

As is often the case with shamans, you don't grasp the entirety of your task until you are in the midst of it. It seemed odd at first that a group of Andean shamans and a band of Western mystics would come together to summon the lightning from the Upper World and bring down a new initiation rite that could benefit all humanity.

I thanked Don Manuel for inviting us, feeling honored that he recognized our readiness for this task.

"I invited you because we needed someone to represent the conquistador, the white man," he explained. "Our people need to heal the wound of the conquest. The raping of our mothers and kidnapping of our children. We need to bury the sword of the conquest."

He paused and looked me in the eyes, and I could see a tear running down his cheek.

"This rite is also for your people," he went on. "You and I are bringing it forth to the world. But neither of us is special—we are simply an instrument of our times."

In that extraordinary expedition that we were fortunate enough to film, the Munay-Ki was born, and I acquired my Andean nickname, Chaka-Runa, the "man bridge." I would become a bridge for an ancient wisdom to a modern time, and the Munay-Ki would be the instrument. You can watch this documentary at www .munay-ki.org.

RECEIVING THE MUNAY-KI RITES

Don Manuel shared all the *karpays,* or initiations, with me, confiding that I was the first non-Indian he had ever brought into his spiritual tradition.

"The karpays are seeds that offer you gifts of power," he explained. "They are like the corn. If you plant the kernels deep inside your heart and water them with your love (*munay*), they will grow and produce great big ears of corn. But you must use this power for good."

As I received Don Manuel's karpays, I noticed how issues I had struggled with for years were starting to resolve. My love and empathy for others were growing. With the more advanced initiations, I began to understand how I could make the world do my bidding and what a high price one had to pay for imposing one's will on life.

I learned how the advanced rites joined you to a lineage of healers and shamans who had defeated death and time and who were available to help you fulfill your mission. There are many of us bridging the ancient wisdom to our modern world, which is sorely in need of a new compass.

Don Manuel encouraged me to help craft the rites for a Western audience, to deliver the wisdom and power that comes with each karpay in a contemporary way. At first we kept to the form in the Quechua language, yet both of us found it cumbersome. My Quechua was embarrassing and his Spanish almost nonexistent. And I wanted to be careful with cultural misappropriation. In that expedition to Mount Ausangate, we agreed to keep the rites as clean and pure as possible, true to their essence. We explained to our students that as you grow your seeds of power, of your "medicine," you are then allowed to offer the rites to others. Your medicine eventually grows to the degree that you are willing to take on the stewardship of Mother Earth and become an Earthkeeper.

The Munay-Ki were designed for a Western audience and seeker. Though I first connected with these initiations with the paqos of the Andes, the Munay-Ki are based on ancient rites found across all cultures. The traditional rites of initiation of the Q'ero belong to them and their children. We must be respectful of the traditions of Andean cultures and considerate of their ways. The Munay-Ki will bring you to the same destiny as the ancient shamanic initiations and allow you to create the new maps of stewardship of Earth that the modern world needs today.

PACHAKUTI AND PACHAKUTEC

Every Andean child has heard the legend of Pachakutec Yupanqui, the son of Viracocha Inka.

When Pachakutec was a young man, the Chanca people were laying siege to the city of Cusco. His father had fled the city, leaving young Pachakutec behind to defend the capitol. Legends say that the sun god Inti responded to the young prince's prayers by turning the stones into warriors, who helped him drive the fierce Chancas back to their villages across the Apurimac River.

Pachakutec is credited with expanding the Inka Empire—the largest kingdom ever known in the Americas, larger in size than the United States—and building cities in the clouds like Machu Picchu, Choquequirao, and Vilcabamba. When he died in the year 1471, he left a prophecy announcing his return to help set the world "right" again. His name means the "earth shaker" or the one who "sets the world right," and many even today believe that he will come back to repair the damage done by the conquistadores.

The name *Pachakuti* refers to the Andean belief of the cyclical renewal of the world. Each cycle brings about creation and destruction. The cyclical nature of the seasons did not escape the sages of old, who believed that the dawn of a "millennium of gold" was near, at the end of the current cycle.

The current Pachakuti started around the beginning of the millennium and foretold changes that would impact all humanity, not only the Andean villagers and their herds of llamas and alpacas. The new cycle would require humans to become Earth stewards instead of Earth parasites. The caring for Pachamama, the Great Mother, would have to become a priority. Only Earthkeepers would survive the coming chaos. A new kind of human would arrive in the world.

HOMO LUMINOUS

The Q'ero were no strangers to the prophecy of the time to come, of the new Pachakuti. Don Manuel Quispe and others believed that they were to play a role in the unfolding of this new time. Don Manuel was one of the last known readers of the *quipu*, a ring of knotted strings on which the stories of the Inka Empire were kept.

And he remembered the legends of when the Inka came from Lake Titicaca, the Sea on Top of the World.

Don Manuel believed that the new caretakers of Earth would come from the West, and he welcomed me heartily when we first met at América's hacienda. "I have been waiting for you for a long time," he said when we first met. I was flattered, yet later I would understand that he was speaking of Westerners and that I happened to be the first one he had encountered.

With Don Manuel I learned that in the realms of magic and mystery, you are in service to a sacred dream that is greater than you are, even as you are an indispensable part of it. You follow the signs of destiny. And Don Manuel was masterful at this. He no longer required logic or reason to compel him to act. This is why he invited 100 of the paqos of Q'ero and their families for our ceremony at Mount Ausangate—to have a meeting with destiny and launch the Munay-Ki.

CREATORS AND CREATION

Don Manuel would not live to see the final rite, the Creator Rite, or the *Taitanchis Ranti* in the Quechua language. We had spoken about it often, about how this rite had existed for millennia among many cultures but was never available to be transmitted person to person. A lightning bolt had to strike you and you had to survive, much like what had happened to Don Manuel. Or a blinding light had to appear to you like with the apostle Paul, when he received the complete Gospel in an instant.

"Our job in this world is to create beauty and peace," Don Manuel once said to me. "The job of creation is not complete as your religions tell. It's up to us to continue to co-create. This is what this rite is about."

My partner Marcela Lobos accompanied me to Mount Ausangate to "bring down" the ninth rite of the Munay-Ki. We were positioned in groups of four, one person facing each of the cardinal directions while we opened sacred space and called on the heavens and the ancient ones to bestow their blessing and wisdom upon us.

Then we began assembling a *despacho*—building a mandala of flowers and grains in a ceremony of gratitude—praying for the ninth rite to be bestowed onto us. I gazed up at the cloudless sky and closed my eyes, surrendering to the quiet for what seemed like an instant, as a soft glacial breeze brushed my face. Suddenly we began to be pelted by hailstones the size of marbles. We all ran toward shelter, hoping our meeting tent would hold up in the storm. Minutes later, as we finished the despacho offering inside the tent, the sky cleared, and the storm departed as rapidly as it had arrived.

That afternoon we all received the Creator Rite and then offered it to each other, Indians and Westerners alike, to anchor its power in our Middle World as we accepted the mandate to become co-creators of beauty and peace.

The Munay-Ki was born here, at Mount Ausangate, and in some strange and mysterious way, it had been preordained.

It's been nearly 20 years since this expedition, and Marcela and I continue sharing the Munay-Ki with our students. I have seen how the Munay-Ki has taken root in her heart and how she has brought a fresh vision of what the rites signify for the Western world. She has the integrity, the ethics, and the love required to articulate their value in these times of need. This is the first time she has shared the rites in book form so that she can reach a wider audience with their powerful message.

Marcela was born in the Andes and lived many years in the United States. She understands the need for this ancestral wisdom to speak to the important global forces shaping today's world.

Marcela's view and offering of the Munay-Ki is deeply grounded in the power of the feminine, in harmony and alignment with the mission offered to her by *Pachamana*, Mother Earth. It did not surprise me then when one day she announced that there was a rite for women, the Rite of the Womb. You will read her story about this rite and how it liberates women from suffering. She will share this extraordinary rite in this book.

The Munay-Ki can help us become the new human announced by the Pachacutti—*Homo luminous*—and this meaningful book will help you get started on your own journey. The rites are profoundly healing, and they empower you to become an agent of change and transformation in the world. The initiations will help turn your deepest wounds into sources of compassion and discover what you came to do and to be on this extraordinary planet. This may be the most important message you ever read.

With munay (love),

Alberto Villoldo, Ph.D.,
founder of the Four Winds Society

THE BEGINNING: RECEIVING MY FIRST MUNAY-KI RITE

There are places where spirits live trapped among stones. Those places, constructed by ancient man and today abandoned, were so sacred that their energies continue to vibrate through the centuries. It is impossible to walk on those stones and not sense the clamor of the past and the enormous force concentrated there.

— ISABEL ALLENDE, *MACCHU PICCHU*

In September 2002, I enrolled in a class that would place me squarely on the path of shamanism. That year, my life had been turned upside down by an imminent separation; as a single mother of two young children, trying to make a living in a foreign country, I was terrified by the unknown future. With a college degree in journalism, I had imagined myself covering news and writing stories from distant, war-torn lands. Little did I suspect the conflict I would be reporting would be from my own home, and it would leave me a broken human after seven years of emotional abuse.

I had to recover my soul.

In June 2003, my mother-in-law agreed to care for my children, and I embarked on a two-week pilgrimage to the Peruvian Andes that I hoped would grant me some respite and help me break free from a life of forced domestication—which had afflicted the women in my family for generations and now hung heavily over me. High in the Andes, I would discover the path to my own healing and the tools to change my life story from victim to hero.

Arriving in Cusco, the ancient capital of the Inka Empire, I was relieved to rest at our hotel to adjust to the altitude and meet my fellow travelers. Each one of us was seeking answers to life's bigger questions: *Why am I here? What is my purpose? How can I contribute to a better world?*

The following day, with two shamans from the Q'ero nation, we rode a bus for a few hours to the trailhead and the start of our five-day trek, in the footsteps of the ancients. The Q'ero are direct descendants of the Inka, the last of a lineage of kings and queens who once ruled the greatest empire in the Americas (from the 13th to the 16th centuries). When I met them, they were still strangers to the Western world; their ancestors had remained hidden from the Spanish conquistadors in high mountain villages, quietly herding their llamas and planting *chuño*, small potatoes that grow at a 15,000-foot altitude, waiting for the ripe moment to deliver their prophecies about the times to come.

The Peruvian Andes rise nearly 23,000 feet; some of these mountains, or *apus* in the Quechua language, are considered sacred guardians of a wisdom that sources from the beginning of life itself. The Andean people still work the soil, living in reciprocity, or *ayni*, with the land. They understand Earth to be the mother, the provider of all nourishment. They live in harmony with the elements: they build their homes from earth, collect water from the streams that flow from melting glaciers, and bask in the light of the sun. As I trekked through the mountains, I could imagine seeing their faces and hearing their voices. The spirits of the ancient Andean peoples still inhabited the land and seemed to act as stewards for the pilgrims who gathered here in search of primordial wisdom.

On this journey, we would be hiking over an icy pass on Salkantay, a mountain whose name means "the wild and untamable"—a truly fitting theme for my journey. After a decade of trying to be a fit housewife, I needed to recover my wild and authentic nature.

As we stepped off the bus, I gazed up at the mountain and thought for sure I would be the first to arrive at the high pass. Since my youth, I had conquered many peaks in Chile, my country of origin, and then in the Wasatch Mountains of Utah. I had been an athlete, scaling summits that most people would find daunting. However, from that first day, I felt off and had a hard time keeping up with the people at the front of the line. It was as if the mountains, as well as Mother Earth, were asking me to slow down and become more receptive to my surroundings.

As we traversed the landscape, the shamans encouraged us to pray to the *apu*, the spirit of the mountain. Every few hundred yards, we would stop to offer *kintus* made from three coca leaves with a flower petal on top. With our breath, we would blow our prayers into each *kintu* and leave it tucked under a rock, asking the wind, the sun, the earth, and the Great Spirit to help us in our ascent. If we felt sadness, anger, or any heaviness, we were instructed to use our breath to blow those feelings into a small stone and later tuck the stone into the earth. To my surprise, I discovered that underneath every feeling of sadness was a tragic story that I had convinced myself was real! "It's simply a belief," a voice inside me would say in response. It was as if the *apu* was whispering to me, instructing me to peel away layers of limiting beliefs and expectations and to release it into the stone I held tightly in my hands.

I could feel myself shedding my identity, but not without tears of pain and grieving. I was letting go of every restrictive thought about what it meant to be a mother and a woman. These included family patterns of mistrust and resentment, social conditioning to be submissive and silent, and other feelings that were beyond words or comprehension. With every step, I deepened my yearning to connect with my own wild, untamable essence—my divine feminine spirit. The glacier's shining presence at night and the roaring of her avalanches under the stars were impossible to ignore, and as each day passed, I felt that I was integrating them into my understanding.

I'd grown up in Chile during a dictatorship, under a regime that was militaristic and steeped in symbols of masculinity. Raised with two brothers, I had found my own strength through physical prowess and intellect. Nevertheless, my parents, who had been gentle and permissive, allowed me to explore what I saw fit. For this reason, ever since the age of 14, I began traveling throughout Chile with friends or on my own. By the age of 20, I had backpacked through Peru, Bolivia, and Ecuador, falling in love with the colorful tapestry of Indigenous life. I walked hundreds of miles of Inka trails from the jungles to the highlands and mountains (days without seeing another a Westerner). I experienced life at its rawest: the rushing waters of rivers, the ever-changing tones of the winds' whistles, colorful weavings, old faces cracked by the weather, young faces with runny noses and hair that had never been combed, and so much more.

I felt the deep mysticism of these places that were so off the beaten path, and I was enchanted. Nevertheless, my call to travel was primarily wrapped around adventure sports, and although I had managed to also surf the Pacific coast in South America, my enthusiasm carried me all the way to California. I was 21 years old when I froze my journalism degree and took off on permanent travels. Ten years later, I found myself in that class offered by the Four Winds Society, which introduced me to the shamanic path and guided me back to the Andes of my youth.

On my second night on the mountain, we were camping right next to the glacier, and my fluffy, warm sleeping bag felt like the thinnest and most transparent skin of an onion. It was one of the most melancholic nights of my life. I spent the night coughing, trembling miserably, and fearing my uncertain future. I felt weak and breathless the following morning as we crossed the pass under a gray sky.

If my ego had previously led me to believe that I could conquer this mountain, the humbling process continued on the third night with an episode of diarrhea. I woke up dehydrated and so weak that I could not walk; instead, I crawled and eventually collapsed and slithered like a serpent while trying to pack my things to move to the next camp. There, belly to belly with the ground, feeling each little rock under my body, I understood for the first time what it was to surrender to the feminine spirit of Earth.

(Eventually, a nurse gave me electrolytes, and once I recovered a little strength, one of our guides walked slowly by my side.)

On this occasion, I did not conquer the mountain; instead, the wild, untamable feminine spirit subdued my brute, masculine determination, until I was quiet enough to feel her deep love. I cried like a baby, and she listened like a mother, reassuring me that my children and I would be okay. Despite the humiliating nature of my experience, I was warmed by the intimacy of this communion.

The hero's journey upon which we embark as a young person can be exciting and even life-changing, but we seldom recognize that the external adventure is merely a representation of the deeper one that is taking place within us. Now I could finally appreciate the outer landscape as a mirror for what I was exploring in the depths of my being. Although I was on a pilgrimage to many sites that had been sacred to Indigenous people, I understood that the true pilgrimage upon which I had embarked was to my own soul.

We were on the other side of the high pass, and the temperature was much warmer as we approached the high jungle around Machu Picchu, the ancient Inka citadel in the clouds. This would be our last evening camping, and it took me by surprise when our lead teacher announced that the two shamans who accompanied us would share a reading of coca leaves about the times to come.

The sun was setting, and we entered a big tent lit by candles set upon fieldstones. We sat gazing intently at the shamans, who seemed to effortlessly carry this timeless practice of divination. Praying to the spirit of the coca plant, they threw a handful of fresh leaves on a cloth to create patterns they would then interpret. The reading was in Quechua and broken Spanish, so some translation was required.

Knowing that I spoke both Spanish and English, the shamans asked me to translate. Soon, the coca leaves were speaking. One of the shamans said, "There is much upheaval to come. . . . There will be raging fires, ice storms, and extreme weather. Mother Earth will cry tears of sadness in the form of tornados, hurricanes, and tsunamis. We have dishonored Pachamama [the Earth goddess the

Andes peoples revere], our loving mother, and as a result, we must face the purification."

My hands were sweating and my heart pounding as I delivered this unsettling message to the others. The shamans kept calling the spirit of the coca with their prayers so they could continue reading the messages from beyond. At the end, they said, "This is the coming of the *pachakuti*, a time when our lives will be turned upside down."

Pachakuti is a Quechua word that literally translates to "turning time/space upside down"; it can also mean "change" or "disturbance." It refers to a period of great transformation and calls for nothing less than a reversal of life as we know it. The time of the pachakuti is an inflection point that signals a change in our way of life. The last pachakuti took place when Spanish conquistadors came to the Americas and wiped out the native populations. The ripple effects were felt around the world, which was never the same afterward, and led in many ways to the state of things today— national boundaries carved by colonization and conquest, the current economic systems and extraction of resources from the land, and globalization and the phantoms it has left in its wake, to name just a few.

Every rite of passage, even if it can open the way to more auspicious times, implies death and rebirth. I held my breath, contemplating how the times to come paralleled the present state of my life.

Our group felt unsettled with all that was shared, and it took me a few moments to recover. However, the shamans continued speaking after chewing coca leaves, as they delved even deeper into the messages from their ancestors and beyond. "If we want to live through these chaotic times, we must come to ayni, the sacred reciprocity with Pachamama and all our relations."

At this point, the Four Winds Society teacher expounded on the opportunity that lay within the prophecies. "Times of crisis are times of great chance," she said. "We must continue to do our personal healing work and prepare to help others when the great upheaval arrives, eventually becoming Earthkeepers and midwives of the times to come on the other side of chaos."

The shamans agreed with our leader that this was an unsurpassed opportunity, and they decided to offer us a transmission known as "the great renewal for the times to come." In Quechua, they spoke about the *Mosoq Karpay*, explaining that it would hit us like a lightning bolt, shattering our outdated beliefs and making room for a new paradigm. *Mosoq* means "new," and *karpay* means "transmission." (Chapter 8 of this book dives into greater detail about this initiation, also known as the Starkeeper Rite, which enables us to make contact with the galactic consciousness.) This initiation was meant to wipe the energetic body clean. It is similar to a baptism, during which the initiate is spiritually purified.

The Mosoq Karpay, one of the rites of the Munay-Ki, invites us to source from the future—from the ones we are becoming. Receiving the rite doesn't automatically lead to our evolution, but if we begin to germinate the seeds of this initiation, we open up and become more attuned to what is coming. We can be liberated from the past and remain alert to what needs to happen in the future.

Receiving this initiation was a powerful experience for me. Soon after the coca leaves had been "read," one of the shamans struck me on the head with a cloth bundle containing small stones. In this Andean tradition, the medicine people anchor their wisdom in stones they find while walking in the mountains during their apprenticeship. They keep these stones wrapped in a cloth woven with the symbols of their cosmology. This bundle becomes their altar or *mesa*, and it is intimately connected to their sacred mountains and to Pachamama. Thus, when I was struck on the head— and later, on the chest and belly—the power of the forces gathered in the medicine bundle was symbolically passed on to me. Finally, when the shaman placed his forehead against my forehead, I was offered the purification and seed of the times to come.

In Andean tradition, the metaphor of transformation is that a seed is planted within the initiate, and it is their tenacity and willingness that enable the seed to grow and flourish. This is akin to bringing down a quantum of the stream of consciousness from the lineage that presides over the specific rite. Because this worldview believes all possibilities already exist within us, the seed that is sown in our field speeds up our evolution toward greater awareness. The dormant possibility that lay within us all this time rises to the surface, and we are given the opportunity to be the person we need to be in order to respond to the challenges in our lives and the world around us. Each transmission of these Andean rites is an empowerment of our own human potential.

Everyone in our tent received the same transmission. The next morning, we began our descent toward Machu Picchu. As we left the glacier behind and entered the warmer forest, my heart opened with excitement and the sense of a new beginning. Everything that would follow was beyond my wildest dreams. The seeds had been planted. I was no longer the same woman I had been only days before.

Returning home from my journey, I realized I was still new to the path of shamanism, yet I was drawn to the system of energy medicine that the Four Winds Society and its founder, Alberto Villoldo, were sharing with Westerners who were tired of living inauthentic lives full of dis-ease and disconnection. I was magnetized by the ancient practices of the Indigenous people of the Andes and Amazon—people who could sense the luminous threads that connect us all. I longed to rediscover the ancient ways of healing. After all, I felt like I was going through my own phoenixlike experience and emerging from the ashes of my past and into a new discovery of who I was.

I would come to learn this body of knowledge in the years after that first pilgrimage as I continued the quest that would lead me into a decade of alchemizing my pain and sorrows into sources of wisdom and compassion. After being initiated into the mystery teachings within the Four Winds Society framework, I learned directly from shamans of the Andes and Amazon. I also returned to Chile, studied with medicine women from the southern part of the country, and created a retreat center in the mountains with Alberto, who became my second husband. I share more details about those years of my quest in my book *Awakening Your Inner Shaman: A Woman's Journey of Self-Discovery through the Medicine Wheel.*

Now, in this book, I invite you to join me in exploring sacred ways to transform your trauma and suffering into wisdom and joy and to understand your place in the cosmos. This is the path of the Munay-Ki: 10 initiations that awaken and empower your own journey toward wholeness and self-realization.

In the Quechua language spoken by the people of the Andes, *munay* refers to unconditional love, and *Ki* is the Japanese word for "power" or "life force energy." Thus, *Munay-Ki* translates to the "power of love" and is meant to activate consciousness toward an embodied and transcendental perception. The essential wisdom of these rites was kept safe for many centuries, and, since the turn of this millennium, has been rapidly spreading to the four corners of the world as we face the collapse of old structures and systems and endure the contractions of birthing a new paradigm.

THE ROOTS OF THE MUNAY-KI

The Munay-Ki belong to a living tradition, meaning they will continue to evolve and grow; however, we pay homage to those who carried the torch of this wisdom before us and to those who continue to walk with us today, in both human and spirit form.

As shared in the Foreword, Alberto first encountered the rites while studying the healing ways of the medicine peoples of the Amazon and the Andes of Peru. He had first approached these traditions from the curious perspective of a medical anthropologist, asking questions such as, "How do these people heal and what are their healing methods?" Soon, he realized this paradigm was not only about healing tools and skills but also about a profound and sacred relationship with nature blended with a fine understanding of how energy works. This was a completely different view from the Western approach that separates the person from the natural environment in the process of diagnosing and "curing" disease. Soon, Alberto became an apprentice for some of the most accomplished medicine peoples from this part of the world.[*]

---

[*]   You can learn more about his teachers and about his personal journey of transformation in his books *Dance of the Four Winds, Island of the Sun,* and *Shaman, Healer, Sage.*

During his apprenticeship, Alberto experienced classical shamanic transmissions from his mentors. In the mountains, his connection was with Q'ero masters who were known to be direct descendants of the Inka nobility that ruled the *tawantinsuyu*, or Inka Empire, between the 13th and 16th centuries. From them, he received initiations that connected not only with the power of nature but also to ancient lineages of healers and Wisdomkeepers. From his time on the coast of Peru, Alberto received the transmission of the seers—those who perceive the energetic essence of reality, beyond physical appearance. And from the jungle, he acquired an intimate relationship with nature spirits (serpent, jaguar, hummingbird, and eagle/condor) that awaken one's own life force potential.

Throughout the years, Alberto cultivated the wisdom offered to him, and with the blessing and the help of his teachers, he shared the transmissions with his Western students. In the long run, what Alberto valued was the essence of the teachings and the potential for awakening that the rites offered. Although he was enchanted with the Indigenous traditions of Peru, he also recognized the opportunity through the lens of a Western academic. He wanted the initiations to fit the context and needs of a 21st-century person in the modern world. Therefore, the Munay-Ki Rites are an adaptation of the colorful transmissions that Alberto received during his training in the spiritual landscapes of Peru.

This new form is not meant to imitate exactly the way the Andean people embody their initiatory rites, and it doesn't require the traditional altar or *mesa*, which can take years to build, or any other items that are distinctive of the Andean tradition.* Indeed, the Munay-Ki are specifically *for* the Western world, which is sorely in need of a new compass and map so it can make its way back to nature and responsible stewardship of Earth.

The writings of this book are sourced from my own experience receiving and cultivating each of the initiations. I also relied on the countless conversations I had with Alberto about the details of each rite and their origins. However, the depths of this work could

---

* In our school, The Four Winds Society, we offer a training in which the students do build a *mesa* and learn more about the Andean cosmology, though it is not exclusively about that. It is an eclectic training that includes other modalities, such as depth psychology, meditation, and neuroscience.

not exist without the hundreds of ceremonies I presided over or attended to during the last 20 years to share the rites with the modern world. Many of these ceremonies happened at sacred sites of ancestral Peru while many other ceremonies took place all around the United States and Europe—often with the active participation of a select few Q'ero paqos who have been vital to the dissemination of these transmissions and who are my point of reference when giving an idea of how the rites live within themselves and their people. Among these individuals are Humberto Soncco, Bernardina Apaza, Francisco Chura, Juana Apaza, Pascual Apaza, and Juan Apaza. From a different village is Porfirio Sequeiros, who also has traveled extensively to offer the rites with The Four Winds Society.

THE EVOLUTIONARY SEEDS

During the times of the Inka Empire, only the main ruler and the nobility were considered Inkas—or children of Inti, the sun—suggesting a primordial superiority to the commoners. With the passing of the centuries, this idea evolved, and today Andean mysticism agrees that all people are born with the Inka seed, the innate capacity to reach the highest spiritual level. Most spiritual traditions convey the same idea—that all humans carry within themselves the potential of complete self-realization, that we are all infinite beings walking Earth in a finite human body.

After 17 years of sharing the rites of the Munay-Ki with thousands of people, I often prefer the metaphor of many seeds rather than just one seed for our infinite potential. This is because we tend to grow and mature certain aspects of ourselves and ignore others. Accordingly, the energetic transmissions of the Munay-Ki either awaken the seeds of our greatest potential if they are dormant, or they empower the seeds if they are already germinating and growing.

The Munay-Ki constitute an embodied path, meaning that the rites encourage us to cultivate the seeds in our day-to-day lives instead of waiting for the wisdom to sprout on its own without any personal effort. This comes about by practicing three key principles from the Andean tradition:

1. *Yachay*—Clear vision and calm thinking
2. *Munay*—Unencumbered love and feelings
3. *Llankay*—Right doing or love in action

I recognize that this may be easier said than done. For this reason, the Munay-Ki are not isolated seeds that came to be like a miracle without any connection to anything else. Of course not! Just as the seeds of nature come from ripened plants or trees, the seeds of the Munay-Ki come from the already mature blueprint of the potential they hold. As you continue reading, you will discover how each *karpay*, or rite, has a clear origin that ripples and trickles toward its destiny in the psyche of the people who receive the initiation and beyond—through the *yachay, munay,* and *llankay* of the practitioner.

While most spiritual traditions preach the importance of transcendence and merging with the unitary light of consciousness, the Munay-Ki guide us to also cultivate an empowered relationship with the dark—understanding it not as something negative but as the fertile grounds from which true power, compassion, and wisdom arise.

People who have journeyed deepest into the land of depression, terror, or death and have managed to return to the light (by not remaining stuck in suffering) tend to exude great compassion, gratitude, ease, and often joy. In this sense, the Munay-Ki empower us to connect with all aspects of ourselves—not only with the lightweight luminous parts but also the heavy and difficult. The seeds of the Munay-Ki take root at the core of our being, in the fruitful darkness of our personal unconscious, in order to nudge us toward a conscious evolution.

THE ANIMATED WORLD

Indigenous traditions across the globe hold the view that all nature—the rocks, trees, skies, oceans, stars, and entire cosmos—is animated or infused with spirit. In other words, everything is filled with consciousness; some phenomena can be more or less conscious, but not separate from the primeval source of consciousness. In the

Andes, they speak about *Kausay Pacha*, the life force that abounds in the Universe and saturates absolutely everything.

In contrast, in modern society, we've inherited the myth of an inanimate world devoid of *anima*, the Latin word for "soul"—specifically, the contemplative and creative feminine aspect of the soul. The result is the objectification and ruthless exploitation of nature and the desecration of life in all the many ways that are driving us to ecocide, the destruction of the natural environment.

Rather than judging the well-being of a society by the health and diversity of nature (including humans), our sick modern systems measure prosperity through the economic abstractions of a market that crushes our morals as well as the world's anima. The incentive for mass consumption, which perpetuates mass production and extraction of Earth's resources, along with the illusion that all this equals prosperity, is part of a vicious cycle that condemns the health and life of all beings on our planet. Humans seem to be the only species that manages to destroy their environment and doom their own destiny.

Nonetheless, humans are not separated from the source of all consciousness and infinite intelligence that creates, destroys, and recreates life. Our essence gives us the potential to envision answers to our crisis (yachay), feel love and compassion as the motivation to make a difference (munay), and invest our energies in manifesting the necessary solutions (llankay).

The Munay-Ki remind us of this vital truth and awaken within us the codes to see, feel, and act in sacred ways while guiding and empowering us to self-realization—from our most infinite and transcendental nature to our humblest and earthiest essence. The rites also serve as a compass that helps us to participate in and even direct the evolutionary quantum age known in the Andes as the *Taripay Pacha* (which translates to "golden age"), prophesied to someday manifest in this terrestrial plane. Rather than simply waiting for the Taripay Pacha to come, we can be audacious and nurture the seeds of our destiny. We can embody and become the new humans our planet needs.

A PATH WITH HEART

The Munay-Ki Rites encompass the initiations you'll learn about in each chapter of this book: the Healer Rite, the Bands of Power Rite, the Harmony Rite, the Seer Rite, the Daykeeper Rite, the Wisdomkeeper Rite, the Earthkeeper Rite, the Starkeeper Rite, and the Creator Rite. I also include a tenth initiation called the Rite of the Womb, which was given to me by a spiritual lineage of medicine women to honor the feminine power to give birth.

In each chapter, I include a detailed explanation of the rite's benefits, how it came to be, and how you can incorporate its wisdom into your own life. While each rite offers a direct transmission of specific qualities from the mentor to the initiate and needs to occur in a ceremonial setting, this book is meant to open your eyes to the many levels of awareness that you can cultivate as well as give you the tools to experience that expansion of your being. You can try all the Practices at the end of each chapter, even if you have not received the rite.

Throughout the practices of each rite, you will learn to awaken your ability to see into the subtle world of energy and spirit; activate the healer within, which will launch you on your own journey of recognizing your innate wholeness; create energetic protections that enable you to walk fearlessly, with grace and discernment; and be connected to a lineage of healers from the past and the future who will guide you and remind you that you are never alone.

These rites do not exist as a hierarchy in which one is more important than another. It is not about climbing a linear ladder to evolution. Rather, the rites complement one another, creating a stronger, more flexible, and more wholesome view of one's existence. Nevertheless, I offer you a default order that has proven to be friendly for the logical mind—as an evolutionary map that can make us excited rather than putting us on guard. It is the same order we have used to give the rites to thousands of students from around the world for over 30 years (though a few rites were incorporated later). Altogether, the Munay-Ki Rites ask us to assume responsibility for our creative power, to move beyond our petty squabbles and destructive tendencies, and to find the wisdom that is necessary to co-create a better world.

Although Alberto received the rites from accomplished Wisdomkeepers who are sometimes considered shamans, I do not want you to think that you need to work with or become a shaman in order to embrace the Munay-Ki. I have intended this book to be a guide for the layperson who wishes to be initiated into a heartfelt evolutionary path that has love at its core. There is no need to do away with your life (family, career, and so on) in order to cultivate your most evolved self. All that is required is your yearning, a little discipline, and integrity.

The Munay-Ki Rites are meant to be simple, accessible, and inclusive. My hope is that this book will open your eyes and heart to the fierce yet gentle beauty and depth of each initiation. It will be an informative guide for those of you who are already on the path and have received the Munay-Ki transmissions—and will show the way for those of you who are only beginning to learn these lessons of awakening and may eventually seek to receive these rites.

If you have been a devotee of a different wisdom tradition, I trust that you will find common ground here, as the Munay-Ki Rites are intended to be complementary to other sacred practices and are ultimately meant to serve your growth. This path is one of many possible, and its beauty will fill you with a sense of wonder for the seen and unseen mysteries of the Universe.

The voices of the lineage of wisdom holders will begin to gently nudge you: "Come here and learn about this," or "Here's a tool that will serve you well." Portals of awareness will open for you. If you feel lost and confused generally as to what should be done, it can be difficult to find such openings. However, as you follow a path of integrity and service, you will discover that the veils between worlds are so thin that you no longer need to seek. Your questions may continue to take you on internal and external voyages of discovery, as mine have, but reality will begin to clearly mirror the answers you are seeking.

One of my first Munay-Ki students, Maria Clara, who is now a teacher of this path, beautifully encapsulated her experience of working with the Rites: "I began to be in tune with life, with the flow of cycles, of preparing the soil, planting the seeds, and eventually the time of harvest and sharing the fruits. I learned to reconcile with my past, heal my fears, forgive, and joyfully embrace an epic destiny that would lead me to self-fulfillment at all levels of my life, not only spiritually but also emotionally and psychologically [with respect to my] health and work."

While the potential for collective evolution is a powerful aspect of these sacred codes, we must start with ourselves. From the perspective of the Munay-Ki, we must continue to "upgrade" our personal software so that we can become more authentic. For example, a person who says they care about Earth but doesn't create the space to connect with nature and doesn't participate in any causes to heal the planet must be intentional about aligning their internal and external realities.

As Mother Earth recycles the old to use as fertilizer for new possibilities to sprout, we have a precious opportunity to make a quantum leap within our own lifetime—to become the new humans prophesied by the ancients. We are bearing witness to the greatest evolutionary leap in history, and we have been given front-row seats—not to watch as passive bystanders as the world unravels but to play an active role in this grand show we call life.

We are beings of cosmic darkness and cosmic light, and we must be ready to serve as peaceful warriors. We can no longer be content to wait for someone else with all the answers to save us or bring us victory. We must summon the strength to be the ones we've been waiting for all along. My hope is that the Munay-Ki Rites will offer you a powerful blueprint for claiming the new human within you who is ready to be birthed in magnificent response to the times to come.

Chapter 1:

THE HEALER RITE

*The process of initiation can be likened to a "sacred catastrophe,"
a holy failure that actually extinguishes our alienation, our
loneliness, and reveals our true nature, our love. That is why
we seek initiation: to heal old wounds by reentering them in
order to transform our suffering into compassion.*

— JOAN HALIFAX, *THE FRUITFUL DARKNESS*

The first Munay-Ki transmission is the Healer Rite, or the Hampe Karpay, and it feels like a natural beginning to become a medicine person. This rite connects us to an ancient and timeless lineage of healers who assist us in our personal transformation and awaken our healing power so that everyone we touch is blessed. We access tremendous spiritual assistance from a lineage that has been holding a seat for us around a sacred healing fire since the beginning of time. These are healers from the past, present, and future who help us address our childhood wounds and those we inherited from our ancestors. They also help us to recognize and heal the collective traumas that keep us in stasis and turmoil.

To be a healer for others, we must know from our own experience how to transform our wounds into sources of wisdom and compassion. The healer lineage accompanies us on our path to harmony and well-being.

According to Jungian analyst Edward F. Edinger, the Greek word *therapeuein*, which translates to "to heal," originally meant "service to the gods."* For the ancients across many cultures, healing occurred in a sacred container. Edinger notes that "a group of pre-Christian, Jewish contemplatives . . . called themselves *therapeuts* 'either because they profess an art of medicine more excellent than in general use in cities (for that only heals bodies, but the other heals souls which are under the mastery of terrible and almost incurable diseases, which pleasures the appetites, fears, and griefs, and covetousness, and follies, and injustice, and all the rest of the innumerable of other passions and vices, have inflicted upon them), or else because they have been instructed by nature and the sacred laws to serve the living God.'"

The notion of healing by the therapeuts deeply resonates with the essence of the Munay-Ki in the sense that it recognizes the spiritual connection of a true healer who is not merely the sum of tools or information gathered lightly in a formal or informal setting. Instead, the authentic healer is aware of the spirit domain and learns the language of energy. Only in this way can a person recognize the works of the lineage coming through their intuition, voice, and hands and allow themselves to be surprised by a feeling or knowing that is beyond their own life experiences.

At the same time, the healer perceives their intimate relationship with nature to the point of knowing that while in a human body, there is no separation—our bones are the minerals, our digestion is fire, and our breath is air. Therefore, besides working as one with the lineage, the Munay-Ki healer operates as one with nature. In the Andes, for example, the *hucha* or heavy energies that can make someone sick are returned to the earth and are replaced with *sami* or nourishing, nectar-like energy that can heal.

As you keep reading about the different rites of the Munay-Ki in all the later chapters, you will see how this awareness of interconnectedness becomes increasingly palpable and clear. Each rite offers a new perspective and abundant possibilities to keep reclaiming our undeniable belonging to Mother Nature.

---

* Edinger, Edwin. *Anatomy of the Psyche.* Peru, IL: Open Court Publishing, 1994.

ORIGINS OF THE HEALER RITE: TRANSFORMING OUR TRAUMA AND ACTIVATING OUR HEALING HANDS

The Healer Rite was initially connected to the idea that the medicine person can alleviate pain or suffering with their hands, meaning they have healing hands. Most of us can recall a time from childhood when we felt pain (from sharp to dull) for whatever reason, and our most instinctive reaction was to place our own hands on the sore spot until a caregiver could come along and relieve us. Often, the adults offered consoling words that had been repeated by their ancestors, as if to activate the healing touch of the hands. In my hometown, the grownups would say, *"Sana, sana, potito de rana; si no sana hoy, sanará mañana,"* meaning, "Heal, heal, little frog's bum; if it doesn't heal today, it will heal tomorrow." You can also think of when you felt emotionally down and someone who cared placed a hand on your shoulder or reached out to hold your hand in theirs.

In hindsight, you will likely recognize that the hands emanate energy and presence, and if someone's heart is pure and their thoughts are positive, they have the potential to transmit a vibration that is soothing. In this sense, the healer is aware of the power of their own vibration and knows that their hands are the means for their intentions. It is common to say that the hands are the direct instruments of the heart.

Now imagine that as a healer you don't have to work alone with your unique gifts, but you have a timeless lineage of healers (from the past, present, and future) who stand by you and offer you an extra hand or many hands when you need it. Then, your healing capacity increases, and you are able to help in deeper ways or reach more people.

Although Alberto first connected with this lineage in the Andes, this is a universal kinship, considering that every community in the world needs healers who remember how to reestablish a person's well-being or balance for the collective. While their expression may vary greatly from one landscape to another—for example, healers from jungles may work more with the waters and plants, while healers from the desert may have to speak with the winds—in essence their work is the same. They remove heavy energies, appease adverse spirits, retrieve lost aspects of the soul, and restore energy flow, each in their own way.

Therefore, when we receive the Healer Rite, we are given the connection to the lineage from the Andes; however, this lineage is linked to all the other lineages of healers, as if they were cousins in a world's family. This is the beauty of receiving the transmission: as healers we don't feel alone. We know that we are standing on the shoulders of those who came before us, and one day we'll be a support for those who are coming after us.

RETRIEVING OUR CONNECTION TO NATURE

In Western culture, we are wounded by an overarching mythology that has existed for at least a couple of thousand years, when the masculine sky god supplanted the feminine deity of Earth, turning her into a subordinate figure rather than a partner in co-creation. Many of these stories are violent allegories for the direction our civilization took, away from harmony and communion with all beings and into a more splintered sense of who we are. The movement toward never-ending "progress," ironically, has at its root a mistaken belief that we have been cast out of the garden due to our sinful nature. That is, we must toil to pay our bills, and we must continually prove ourselves because we secretly (or not so secretly) believe that we are inferior and separate from everything else. We live in a world that became increasingly disassociated and disconnected from nature—from the rhythms, seasons, and cycles of Earth.

Of course, this attitude could not go on forever without us facing the highest price. Our own survival is at stake in the midst of a mass extinction crisis (the rapid and widespread decrease in biodiversity) that is costing the lives of thousands of species each year.[*]

---

[*]   Experts estimate the rate to be between 1,000 and 10,000 times higher than the natural extinction rate (which is for natural reasons when humans were not an influence).

It is not a mystery, then, why so many people are feeling the call to become healers or stewards of life in one way or another. How can we keep going through the motions of working to consume the vital foundations for our livelihood without renewing those resources? This imperative question at the heart of today's human existence is exactly what makes the Munay-Ki philosophy and rites immensely timely.

The notion of ayni, or reciprocity, is the guiding principle for the earth-based traditions of the Quechuan Andes. At a more superficial level, it means "today for you and tomorrow for me," speaking about the generous disposition to help one another within a community. However, it also signifies gratitude for all that Spirit and Mother Earth offer so we can exist and be ready to serve life according to our own capacity. As I wrote in my previous book, *Awakening Your Inner Shaman,* ayni is not a mathematical equation, but rather a spiritual one. Only the individual knows in their heart how much they have given in relationship to their own abilities, and only Spirit can keep record of each person's heart.

The way the Healer's rite is transmitted reflects the importance of connecting with nature. First, the person offering the initiation touches the head, heart, and belly of the initiate with a prayer to align those three centers with the wisdom of the heavens, mountains, and land respectively. The hands are activated next with the giver's intention to connect the protégé with the lineage.

The path of the Munay-Ki awakens our appreciation for the precious gift that is life and kindles our commitment to be its stewards. It teaches us how to cultivate ayni with nature and all our relations and how to flow with the sacred cycles that renew life, from decay and death to rebirth and maturation. We learn to say yes to the calling we hear within to care for life in our precious planet Earth.

HEALING BEGINS AT HOME

Once we receive the Healer's Rite, or feel the commitment to activate our hearts and hands, then we discover that we are most effective when we embody the verb "to heal." This means healing is not something we *do*, but it's who we *are*. It is our commitment to strive toward equilibrium so that no part of the self goes neglected. It implies a daily practice, an attitude, and a perspective on life. Only in this way can we endure helping others, instead of reaching a point in which our energies run dry. We have all met people whose presence exudes peace and comfort, and simply being with them feels refreshing or soothing. In the meantime, there are those who might have great intentions of helping, but just being around them feels nerve-racking or heavy.

Having studied massage therapy in my late twenties, and having received massages from some of the best hands around the world, I can always tell who is applying pure technique with minimum awareness of their own life force and those who are aware of their own breath and connection to nature while treating. If the technical aspect is similar in both cases, the second type of person is always more effective in helping to relieve my tension.

The healer who embodies self-care chooses to see their own body as a temple for the soul, a vessel for the entirety of their being. This can quickly result in adopting a healthier diet, exercising regularly, and resting more while creating healthy boundaries, cultivating meaningful friendships, and avoiding stress if at all possible. I know how difficult this can be for a parent with young children, not enough money, and too many responsibilities. However, this is the reason the Healer Rite invites you to look at your own limiting beliefs so that regardless of the outer conditions, you can begin your healing journey—and ultimately transform your wounds and weaknesses into medicine and strength that can be shared. To be a healer for others, we must know from our own experience how to alchemize our pain and sorrow into sources of light and wisdom.

THE WOUNDED HEALER

For me, the Healer Rite is a reiteration of the commitment we make to ourselves to embark on the medicine path. And of course, while it may seem daunting at first, we can take solace in the lineage that accompanies us, guides us, lets us know when we need to turn left or right, and informs us about what is too much or too little. It helps us develop an instinct about the right place for us to be and which medicine to cultivate. Of course, we each need to discover the unique medicine within ourselves that we are meant to offer others.

As we keep exploring what healing is, it is useful to consider the archetype known as *the wounded healer* (an idea first put forth and explained by Jung). It refers to someone who uses their own experiences of suffering and personal struggle to develop greater empathy for others. In our willingness to delve into our own reserves of sadness, rage, fear, and inadequacy, we learn to recognize and empathize with others who may be going through similar experiences. By learning to be present with ourselves, we learn to be present for others who may recognize they are not alone as they transmute their pain.

Many wounds can be healed, but some wounds may never leave us in this lifetime, no matter what we do. This is part of the healer's journey: to be with that hurt and pain, that situation that pierces us to our core, even as time passes. It is not a linear journey, and we are meant to source our compassion and patience to make the most of a difficult situation. Instead of despairing that we haven't made progress or complaining about this part of ourselves, we dive deeply into our wounding so we may understand it better and eventually make it our ally.

Sudden and permanent healing is not our goal. No, for we are human, *humus* (the organic component of soil), earth itself. We are not meant to be unsullied and flawless! Instead, these places of pain require us to love them until we can hear them speak and tell us what they've come to teach. These vulnerabilities can help temper our being with humility, appreciation, and a greater capacity to make peace with the mystery of life—to learn to dance with it rather than attempting to control every aspect of our evolution.

As wounded healers, before focusing outward on lofty dreams of world peace and oneness, we devote ourselves to our own healing and awakening. The work is in showing up every day and addressing what needs to be addressed. It is similar to the Zen saying, "Before enlightenment, chop wood and carry water. After enlightenment, chop wood and carry water."

And the Munay-Ki Rites will do just that. We come as we are—but be prepared. Receiving these initiations will bring up everything that needs to surface and be addressed. All the cobwebs and dust from the dark corners of our lives—everything that is no longer serving us or needs to be mulched within us—will come up for healing with these transmissions. This is mainly so that we can be the clearest conduit, capable of seeing the soul of the world instead of our own narcissistic projections.

CLAIMING OUR HEALING HANDS

One of my students, Katrin, shares her powerful story of releasing the burden of ancestral trauma and claiming the gifts of her own healing hands, freed from her ancestor's guilt. Although Katrin's journey includes a sojourn with plant medicine, her realizations mirror the process of the Healer Rite, which enables us to take accountability for our own healing process and recognize the ways in which our boundaries must be reshaped to hold our own experience, and not that of the previous generations.

> *I had met a shaman in Cusco, Peru, who had consulted the coca leaves to find out if San Pedro was the right medicine for me and what dosage would be right. And so here I was, in a nice and quiet B&B with a sheltered garden in the beautiful Sacred Valley. I had decided to do the ceremony here, knowing that the owners of the place (and experienced medicine people) would be holding space for me.*
>
> *It was a warm and sunny morning when I leaped into this new experience. I opened sacred space and summoned my helpers in the spirit world before drinking the medicine in one go. Slowly, my perception changed, and I became very relaxed. I lay down, enjoying the soft grass and the warmth of the sun. I melted into what felt like just being.*
>
> *After what seemed like hours, I had the urge to look at my hands. I observed them very carefully, as if I were seeing them for the first time. I knew that these were healing hands—and I got very sad when I once again realized that I didn't trust them. There was an energy attached*

to them that made them feel "crippled." Suddenly, feelings of deep sadness, guilt, and fear washed over me. I found myself sobbing helplessly, a stream of tears running down my cheeks. I was in total despair and close to panicking. I was gasping for air and felt as if all oxygen was being pressed out of my lungs. The physical sensations were very strong.

In all this, I managed to stay focused while looking at my hands. What was this about? It felt as if the feelings I experienced belonged to someone else . . . and so I asked Spirit if she could help me. Suddenly, my grandfather appeared in my mind's eye. He was sitting in a trench in World War II, all alone, dirty, exhausted, and very frightened. He was looking at his own hands in disbelief. He was in utter despair. My grandfather was a doctor, serving in different military hospitals in World War II. The "official" story told in our family was that he was so passionate about serving his comrades that he turned down an offer to return home from Prague to Austria with his young wife and their first child (my mother) in the summer of 1944. What might have supported his choice of staying in the battlefield was the fact that he was a member of the Armed SS (Schutzstaffel), the paramilitary unit that was most responsible for the genocide in the Holocaust, bringing terror and death wherever they roamed. And there he was . . . my mother's father, who went missing without any notice, who never returned home. He looked so tired, helpless, and in agony. I realized he was looking at his hands like I was looking at mine—grandfather and granddaughter united in the same overwhelming emotions.

It was then that I realized that what I felt belonged to him—I felt his feelings! His despair was about three things: First of all, it was about not being able to help everyone . . . he felt like he needed to rescue everyone and was completely weighed down by this burden! Second, he was afraid of failing and of harming or even killing someone. The third emotion he had passed on to me was guilt, and this one made me gasp for air. I realized that this was exactly what had paralyzed me for years working as a midwife!

I felt I needed to do something about it and decided to ask my grandfather if he was prepared to take back what he had handed over to me in order to fulfill what he hadn't been able to (when he was alive). I wrapped up all that was connected to our common experience into what looked like a little parcel. We looked into each other's eyes and found love, compassion, understanding, and forgiveness. I explained to him that my hands were healing hands, just like his, but that they were heavy with a *guilt that wasn't mine and debilitated with fear and exaggerated expectations that I presumed were his. He listened attentively and nodded. I felt the love he felt for me, and for a brief moment, we felt the sadness of never having met in person. He reached out, and I placed the parcel in his hands, giving him back what belonged to him. We shared a moment of silence and said good-bye.*

The Spirit of San Pedro was very kind and gave me a break. Pachamama held me and hugged me with her warm surface; Father Sun warmed me with his powerful rays and bathed everything in an incredibly bright and soothing light. When I woke up again, the healing journey continued. I looked at my hands, and there came another wave of tears and sadness that went on for some minutes. And then, suddenly, all the weight was lifted, and I saw my hands beaming with energy! They were glowing and pulsating, and I felt a surge of power running through them. I felt their tremendous healing qualities—for the first time, without the weight of the fear and expectations that had controlled me for so long. I looked at them in amazement . . . turned them around . . . touched the grass . . . and enjoyed the lightness and beauty of the experience.

My hands feel very different, and so does my whole being. I received a very deep healing that I'm very, very grateful for. I know that this experience is a gift and that it will have a deep impact on my personal and professional life.

Just as it happened for Katrin, assisted by the Spirit of the San Pedro cactus (*Echinopsis pachanoi*), the healer's lineage guides us to immerse ourselves on our personal healing journey of transforming our wounds into medicine. The Healer Rite reconnects us to our hearts and hands, to Mother Earth and the heavens, and to our full humanity; we begin to remember who we are in the entirety of our essence, from bones, blood, tears, and hair to our infinite and luminous selves.

The beautiful thing about this initiation is that it does not require us to relinquish any part of ourselves. We do not try to transcend our physical bodies as if they are hindrances, nor do we become mired in our limitations. We are simply invited into a greater sense of awe and humility as we consider the full scope of what we contain.

SETTING DOWN THE CROSS

Through the next story, I invite you to reflect on how helping others doesn't mean carrying their burdens—their proverbial cross, so to speak—at least not forever. Instead, it is about holding the kind of reverential space that makes healing possible. It is every person's sacred duty to seek their own healing as the healer holds space and the vibration to facilitate this process.

A few days after I turned 50 years old, while in ceremony with healers from the jungle, I unexpectedly had a vision and a feeling that my father's legs were cold. Intuitively, I rubbed my hands for a few seconds to create heat and then energetically placed them along his legs. While repeating this same motion a few times, it occurred to me that it would be better to connect him with the lineage of healers so he could be guided and assisted in his healing and not keep depending on me.

Over the next few minutes, my thoughts kept unfolding until I realized that I had been carrying the weight of his cross all my life. He is a good man, but like every human, he's made mistakes, and some of his mistakes were very costly to my family. But because I love my father so much, as a child I began carrying the cross of his errors for him, and now I could see that I had been doing it for decades, without even knowing it. Suddenly, this cross felt very heavy on my back, and I understood that this was no longer right.

Although over the years I had worked so much on releasing toxic ties to my family, loosening this cross was happening at a deeper level, thanks to the powerful presence of the lineage of healers. Of course! Why not trust the lineage to help my dad?

Since my father lives right in front of the beach, I visualized myself tossing this cross deep into the ocean. What a great liberation! Then I invited my father's soul to receive the transmission, and I prayed to the lineage to accompany him through the rest of this life and beyond. I could finally release my father into his own destiny, knowing he would have guidance for his own healing journey.

Once we awaken to the realization that no one can really take the journey for us and that we ourselves must walk through the flames of transformation, we accept the invitation from Spirit. If we are on a healing journey, we recognize that being human will bring its fair share of challenges, and that there will always be something for us to work on. As long as we allow ourselves to fully confront our inner agony and examine the pain that lingers in our shadow, we do the inner alchemy of turning the lead of our suffering into the gold of our awakening. As healers—especially if we are conditioned to take on the emotional burdens of others— we must remember that being of service does not mean shouldering their burden. At some point, they will have to take back their load and feel its weight; it is up to them to transmute the cross they bear. Nonetheless, we can always entrust the lineage to help our loved ones to heal and transform their suffering instead of taking it on ourselves.

THE HEART OF THE HEALER

As we bring this lineage of healers out of the Andean setting to varied landscapes, including the world of steel and concrete, the expression of the rite evolves to meet contemporary needs. There is no one-size-fits-all path for the healer.

After receiving this transmission, and once the seeds begin to germinate, there is an endless array of pathways available to us. For ancestral societies, a lot depends on their traditional way of practicing as well as the element that may be calling out to them. For example, healers from the Andes—where people graze vicuñas and grow potatoes in the high mountains—are masters at creating rituals for the health of their animals and for an auspicious harvest. Meanwhile, a healer from the Amazon might spend a lifetime learning about medicinal plants while being able to track forward and backward the story of someone using the metaphor of the river (upriver is the source and downriver is destiny).

The different environments shape the way healers develop their tools and techniques. In the modern world, where we are most disconnected from the natural environment, there is an emphasis on clinical analysis and treatment, often ignoring the soul aspect of life. However, as healers in the way intended by the lineage, no matter what healing modality one chooses—bodywork, psychotherapy, medical doctor, and so on—we are bringing not only the techniques but also our own caring heart.

Being a healer with heart requires *presence*. Thus, the Healer Rite encourages us to first be present with all aspects of ourselves: to show up compassionately with all that hurts and to be grateful for all our strengths, to honor the body, to alchemize our heavy emotions, and to listen to our spiritual needs. Then we can be a true healing presence for others, no matter what we do for a living. In this sense, it is not about what we do for a job. It is about our heart being awakened to see others as they truly are, just as we see ourselves, in all our joys and pains and sadness and potential. This is what it means to show up with the heart of a healer.

Still, in the chaotic times that we are living, it is crucial to find the support for our healing journey. Acknowledging our blind spots is a great step. Asking others to help us recognize what is really difficult to see about ourselves is a strength and not a weakness. It means we accept our vulnerabilities and that we are humble to accept that we don't know everything. Of course, we have to be mindful about whom we ask and choose someone who is also clear and honest about their own limitations.

In this way, just as we reach out to the spiritual and ethereal aspect of the healer's lineage, we must seek the embodied support in any aspect that is difficult for us to face alone. This is how we also honor the great web of love and intelligence that we all are. Helping each other heal and remember how to go about life is the most natural and organic thing to do—it makes us be what we truly are: interconnected beings that desperately need to acknowledge each other with an open heart if we are to survive these times of great change and mass extinction (more on this in the next chapters).

Practice: Create a Mandala—
a Symbolic Mirror of Your Psyche

Creating a mandala is a meditation, a path to inner wisdom, and it can be a powerful tool for healing and transformation. The word *mandala* means "circle" in Sanskrit, and it uses symbols to represent a macrocosm in a microcosm. For this reason, we create a mandala to mirror our present state of being while contemplating the latent possibilities of our life's journey and ultimately acting in the way that feels most authentic.

Hopefully, you create the mandala outdoors; otherwise gather your items from nature and then move indoors. First determine where you are going to make your symbolic circle and then go for a walk in nature and gather items that call to you. Trust yourself; you will be drawn to elements that symbolize the issues you might be addressing (navigating grief, finding your voice, establishing a sense of purpose within your community, and so on). Typically, these include items such as stones, twigs, leaves, and flowers; or they can be grains or seeds. While collecting these items, be mindful of the spirits of nature, speak your intention and say thank you, especially if you are taking from a living plant. You may also include a personal object that has a particular meaning to you.

When you are ready, sit comfortably next to the place where you are going to build the mandala and set your intention. Bring your hands in front of your heart and call the lineage of healers to assist your process. You may also invoke Spirit or Mother Nature in any way that feels authentic to you. Pray to be protected and guided. Then begin forming the circle with some of your collected items. This circle will be the container of the elements representing your inner world. Take a few conscious breaths and continue placing the rest of the items within the circle. Don't think about it; just allow your intuition to direct the work of choosing and arranging the items. If there is something in your conscious mind that you want to add because it feels pertinent to your healing journey, you can pick a representation. Perhaps a prickly fruit can be an image of the wounds you carry, an acorn can mean an important relationship, and a special stone might feel like a symbol of your essential self. There are no rules; just make sure it feels authentic.

When your mandala appears complete, study your creation, paying close attention to the emotions and insights that come to you. You may feel the need to remove or rearrange some of the items—in essence, remapping your energy. Go ahead. This desire for change represents transformation and healing, and you will likely feel different afterward.

Once you are done, leave it as it is for at least three days and visit it at least once a day. Each time, bring any new items that speak to you and remove or rearrange as you see fit. You may wish to journal about your reflections. Overall, the work with the mandala allows transformation as we move the elements of our psyche toward greater coherence and therefore toward greater well-being.

In the end, dismantle the mandala and scatter the elements on the ground or give them to a river or to a bonfire (make sure it is safe). Give thanks to the Great Spirit, Mother Nature, and the lineage of healers for assisting you.

Chapter 2:

THE BANDS OF POWER RITE

*The sediments of the earth make up our cells, and the briny oceans
flow through our veins and tissues. Our ancestors storied this deep
knowing into tales of the community of nature: the marriage of heaven
and earth; the churning of the ocean to create the nectar of life; the
action of the wind upon the waters to bring form out of chaos.*

— JEAN HOUSTON, *THE PASSION OF ISIS AND OSIRIS:
A GATEWAY TO TRANSCENDENT LOVE*

As we explored in the last chapter, the first initiation connects
the initiate to a lineage of healers. The second, third, and fourth
rites of the Munay-Ki, which we will delve into in the next three
chapters, are energetic installations that wake up and enhance the
body's natural intelligence. They give us protection, awaken dormant instincts, and offer a more holistic vision—all for the purpose of preparation, to aid us in becoming medicine people. For
this reason, they are known as technical rites rather than rites that
connect us to lineages.

The second Munay-Ki transmission, the Bands of Power, or
Chumpi Karpay (*chumpi* is the Quechua word for "belt" or "band"),
offers protection by organizing each element—earth, water, air,
fire, and pure light—as an individual energetic belt around the
body of the person who is being initiated. This strengthens our

connection to nature, reminding us of her infinite wisdom and power. Each element is vital for our existence and can germinate and feed life but also destroy and compost what no longer serves. They help stimulate an auspicious ecosphere for our body, and they act as filters that break down heavy energies, thus protecting us physically and psychically.

Alberto first received the Bands of Power from his friend and colleague Juan Nuñez del Prado, a renowned teacher of Inka mysticism whose father was one of the first anthropologists to visit the Q'ero nation. However, these bands do not originate from within the Q'ero communities but from another source in the Andes. On that occasion, the bands were installed using alabaster stones with points representing essential life principles. One point refers to the oneness of the Universe; two points refer to duality or complementary opposites; three points to the Lower, Middle, and Upper Worlds; four points to the cardinal directions of south, west, north, and east; and five points to the elements (earth, water, fire, air, and pure light) and the principle of transcendence—the fifth world into which we are emerging as *Homo luminous*, according to Alberto.

Since the Munay-Ki path keeps to the essence, instead of focusing on the outer form, we use only one stone known as the *Pi stone*—a circular stone with a hole in the middle that is found all over the ancient world, from Asia to the Americas. The Pi stone is full of symbolism, including wholeness and the eternal cycle of life and death. For the Munay-Ki, it also represents the gateway from the material dimension to the world of spirit and vice versa. It is the portal through which we receive the energetic transmission of the rites. (In the Appendix of this book, you will find more information on how to work with the Pi stone through the whole Munay-Ki process.)

ORIGINS OF THE BANDS OF POWER RITE:
WEAVERS AND FARMERS

Juan also shared with Alberto the poetic meaning behind the words and intention used while installing the bands. Because the Andean peoples are weavers and farmers, the Bands of Power are symbols of their everyday lives.

These people have been avid weavers for millennia. Textiles dating from more than 6,000 years ago have been discovered in the Andes, thanks to the extremely dry conditions of the Peruvian high desert. We know that many of these surviving textiles come from funerary bundles, but they encompass a range of purposes, from ceremonial clothing, to armor, to knotted fibers for record keeping. We also know today that these weavings were of deep cultural significance and were often exchanged between groups of people for political negotiation and diplomacy. The textiles communicated everything from social status and wealth to tribal and regional affiliations. The fact that the textiles were so much a part of the Andean cultures is in large part due to the belief that the symbols and materials used were infused with spiritual significance.

To this day, weaving is an essential part of the Andean peoples, and it's not unusual to encounter men, women, and children spinning wool or knitting their traditional clothing and ceremonial attire. Thus, when speaking about the Bands of Power Rite, it is natural to speak about weaving the elements around the body as a series of bands or belts and knotting them in place with the golden and silver energetic threads that run up and down the spine and are our connection to the moon and sun. In yoga, the channels on either side of the spine are known as Ida (representing the yin or feminine energies of the moon) and Pingala (representing the active or masculine energies of the sun). When the flow of these channels is disrupted, we experience depletion and disconnection. However, when the proper protections are put in place, we experience a robustness of body, mind, and spirit.

The Bands of Power also symbolize the stages of growth of a seed, which germinates inside the dark, moist earth, is nourished by the waters, and is fed by sunlight. After the plant matures and bears fruit, the wind carries its seeds to a broader landscape, and it eventually returns to white light with death and the changing of the seasons.

The Andean people mastered the art of farming at different elevations, from close to sea level on the jungle floors to more than 15,000 feet in their mountain villages. Eight thousand years ago, they domesticated potatoes, and with time, created more than 4,000 varieties, ranging from small, white, and round to large, curvy, and purple, and everything in between. Since antiquity, they have also produced quinoa, amaranth, and dozens of different breeds of corn. Thus, the rite has emerged from people who have lived in collaboration with nature, akin to gardeners who never left Eden but who maintained a seamless connection with the elements in all their activities.

In this sense, the Munay-Ki speaks about sowing the seeds of our dreams and nurturing those dreams until they offer the fruits that represent transcending our "needy little me" consciousness to embody the generous "all of us," with an awakened heart and mind. Therefore, with the bands we create a fertile personal ecosystem in which to cultivate our dreams.

THE FIVE COLORS AND FIVE ELEMENTS OF THE BANDS

The first band of protection is energetically woven horizontally around the belly and lower back. It is black in color, resembling the fertile, nutrient-rich earth element—a perfect ground to sow the seeds of who we want to become. The second band, netted around the body at the solar plexus, is created with the water element. It is red in color, representing the vital essence of blood that nourishes the seeds of our becoming. The third band is woven around the heart area with the golden light of fire whose heat germinates the seeds and makes them grow to higher realms. At the throat level, the fourth band is placed, summoning the air ele-ment that is tinged by the brilliant silver that shines under the moonlight. Once the seeds of healing that have been planted have borne fruits, these fruits birth seeds that the winds of this band will carry to new fields, thus rippling the reach of our intentions and deeds. The fifth band is white and is woven like a headband at the forehead, purifying and activating our seeds and creations, just as the Great Spirit shines love and consciousness upon us.

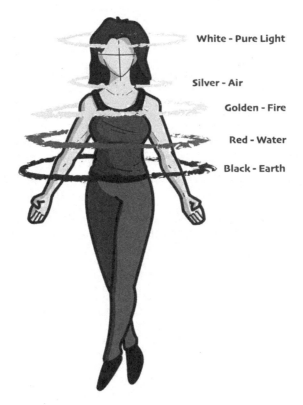

During the initiation process, the shaman organizes the ele-ments one at a time in a circle around the body, beginning with the earth and moving all the way up to pure light. In general, shamans recognize the elements as the building blocks of life, meaning they exist in every single person. Essentially, we are no different from rivers, volcanoes, clouds, earth, fields, or any other expression of the elements. Thus, when shamans are summoning the elements, they are not simply calling for some external source of energy; they are also summoning a quantum of the elemental energy that already lives within us. This emphasizes the connection between the ecosphere (the biological domain of our bodies and our planet) and the noosphere (the domain of consciousness). As ancient alchemists knew, "As within, so without; as above, so below," meaning the internal world is a reflection of the external, and vice versa. Thus, each band strengthens our sense of belonging to nature and of carrying nature's fortitude—including its purifying and rejuvenating qualities.

RECEIVING INTERNAL AND EXTERNAL PROTECTION

When we receive this rite, our system begins to offer itself a sense of protection and healing. We experience the areas where we have built defenses around our hearts and bodies, and in the form of the *chumpi*, we receive an antidote. After all, the earth band is not only available to help us sow the seeds of our longings but also to compost what has died or needs to die within us. In a similar way, the water band cools off our solar plexus when the hepatic system (the part of the body that detoxifies blood) is overrun by heat from stress and toxic foods, which can result in anger, moodiness, headaches, a flushed face, insomnia, and other emotional and physical disorders. The golden band of fire can warm up the sadness and melancholy of our hearts and the dampness in the lungs, which allows us to prevent and clear fungal and bacterial infections. The air band can be activated as wind to help us vocally express our being while clearing the trauma of having been unable to yawn, hum, whistle, scream, sing, or speak our truth. The pure white light band illuminates our thoughts and clears our sight while expelling negative thinking. In this way, the elements coalesce to quell the disturbances of the body and spirit . . . to clear the obstacles that may be preventing a free flow of energy within us.

Further, the bands protect us not only from ourselves but also from external circumstances. When negativity comes our way, it will first touch the bands, which act like a filter that breaks down dense energies into the five elements: earth, water, fire, air, and pure light. The heavy energy is transformed and becomes something that the body can simply compost or absorb as nourishment. In many ways, illness does not necessarily come from a weak physical body but a weak energetic body, which the bands have the power to strengthen. If we find ourselves feeling negativity or heavy energies, we can activate the bands to expel those energies away from us. (Details on how to expand and then rotate the bands at a great speed are specified on the munay-ki.org website.)

Of course, none of these benefits occur magically or overnight. The elements truly aid us in reestablishing harmony and balance in our bodies and psyches, but aside from receiving an initiation from a Munay-Ki practitioner, it is also important that we actively work and meditate with the bands (be sure to review the Practice section for further details).

In subtle ways, the Bands of Power aid us in becoming more present and available for life instead of squandering our energy on fear, doubt, or worry. Experiencing the bands equals remembering that we are not alone in the world, and that we are one with Mother Nature. It also means that we can access the wisdom of the elements anytime we summon their qualities.

PROTECTION THROUGH CONNECTION

When I talk about the bands offering us protection, it is different from the defenses that we tend to build when we experience the world in an adversarial way. The *chumpis* are not the same as the rigid armor we have placed around ourselves to emotionally protect us from other people in the wake of being hurt. When we experience great pain—for example, a breakup or disappointment—we might say, "I will never again open my heart as fully or quickly with anyone else." We start making these contracts with ourselves, even if they create a sense of isolation and become self-fulfilling prophecies that we fall back on so that we never need to take the risk of loving and being hurt. Our internal dialogue becomes self-defeating ("I knew he could never love me"; "If anyone cares about me, there must be something wrong with them"; "It's safer to be alone"), which curtails our naked, natural, immediate connection with others. It also prevents us from being able to access the healing powers of the elements; we are not separate from nature, but the walls we erect keep its palliative effects at bay.

The defenses we build around ourselves usually originate from the painful events in our lives. We created stories out of these moments that resulted in truncating our emotional response or numbing our truth. But, of course, this doesn't make us safe or happy. It is akin to erecting a high tower around ourselves, one built from our conviction that we will "never again" be hurt in the same ways we were before; in the meantime, a protective moat full of alligators surrounds us on all sides. The vacant rooms in our tower fill with regret and sorrow, and infinite possibility seems like a pipe dream—something only in fairy tales. We then make associations to ease and justify our pain, like "love is abuse," or "men can't be trusted," so we never have to open our hearts fully.

Walls can come in a variety of forms, from emotional withdrawal to self-deprecation (after all, if we reject ourselves before others have the opportunity to do so, we feel safer) to physical armor that hides our vulnerabilities. For example, those of us who dabble in multiple cosmetic enhancements, from surgery to antiaging creams, can reflect on the deeper motives besides wanting to look good. Are we bathing in an idealized version of a former self and the fear of losing what we once had or what could have been? Our protective walls keep us stuck and disconnected from the healing and regenerative powers of nature. We abandon our naked, natural, primal selves in order to forget the disappointments of the past and feel some sense of security, even in our discomfort.

I remember a woman who came to one of my women's journeys and wore a lot of makeup—especially heavy black eyeliner around her eyes. As the women began to build trust with each other, we asked her if she would remove her makeup, so we could see who was behind that mask. She replied, "In 30 years, I have never gone out in the world without this makeup. It makes me feel too vulnerable to do so." However, she did reveal herself without the makeup and that was the beginning of a great healing journey.

Wherever we feel vulnerable, we create strategies that enable us to hide—even to scare others so we can keep them away. The Bands of Power will help us dismantle these defenses. Instead of anticipating defeat and reacting from a place of fear, the bands help us connect with our courage to navigate the difficult moments of our lives without fighting, fleeing, or freezing. The elements, from earth to light, help us gather the protective energy that will best serve us, including setting boundaries or a "don't mess with me" vibe when we are about to enter a potentially dangerous situation. As we feel protected and safe in our own bodies, surrounded by the benevolent support of the earth, the old walls gradually crumble.

MAINTAINING AN OPEN HEART AND A HEALTHY FLOW OF ENERGY

One of the most beautiful aspects of the Bands of Power is that they infuse you with a sense of courage and a deeper trust in yourself and the Universe, even in the face of potential conflict or experiences that might summon old wounds. They give us greater behavioral flexibility, meaning they fortify our systems so that we can make new choices from our authentic self, not the reactive patterns that may have constricted our aliveness in the past. The Bands of Power show us that we are part of a much larger ecosystem that encompasses nature, the cosmos, and the Great Spirit and is manifested in the mundane and extraordinary facets of our lives—and all this is here to support us and encourage our full self-expression.

Karen, who is a dear Munay-Ki teacher, experienced this notion firsthand after receiving the Bands of Power during a candlelit ceremony in Park City, Utah, in 2005. While she would later note how beautiful and meaningful the ritual was, she also admitted that she had no idea at the time how important it would come to be in her life. She says:

As weeks passed and I cultivated my awareness of these protective bands, I noticed a new feeling of safety in my own skin, like I was being held in a cocoon of rainbow light. I lived on 40 acres, away from town, and on snowy nights when my snowmobile wouldn't start, I had to walk a half mile to my house. While I felt very connected to nature and knew the land intimately, on moonless nights, the sound of coyotes or bobcats nearby could be unsettling. On those nights, when I envisioned the bands expanding around me, I became one with this natural world, and the fear that once made me look over my shoulder in the past vanished.

As my connection with these bands and with my energy field deepened over time, it became second nature to activate them at any time—in a crowded venue of strangers, before stepping into an uncomfortable situation, or walking through the bustling streets of a city.

The bands protected me in a particular situation with my estranged brother, who lived on the same property but refused to be in my presence. One day, my mom called, extremely concerned about his safety, and asked me to check on him, though she knew I risked being the target of his anger and fury if he were home. Genuinely concerned for his safety, I agreed to go, despite our troubled relationship. As I drove up the road, I stopped and expanded my bands around me, calling in help. This rainbow cocoon surrounded me as I stepped out of my car and approached the door.

Keeping my bands expanded, I knocked on his door and was immediately relieved to see that he was okay. His looming figure opened the door and, as I knew he would, he demanded to know why I was on his property. This time was different—his anger and venom seemed to slip right off me. I told him why I was there and asked if I could give him a hug. He allowed me to do this, although with the caveat that I never ask again. As I left and returned to my house, I was so grateful for the bands and how they allowed me to keep my heart open in spite of the anger and resentment being hurled at me at close range. I didn't need to try to rekindle a relationship with my brother—his pain and hurt were too deep and the walls too thick—but I could easily feel compassion for him and for myself.

In my work in the field of addiction and trauma, this rite has been a gift to many of my clients who have needed support as they begin to dismantle the protective armor that they put on layer by layer from a life of wounding, just like my brother. It has been my honor to share this rite with many and to have the blessing of seeing it bring change to individuals, just like it did for me.

TRUE HARMONY WITH THE ELEMENTS

A key concept that we can glean from the Bands of Power is being in harmony with the elements for our healing and thriving in this life. In the Western world, our disconnection with nature began even before the Industrial Revolution of the 19th century, which focused on efficiency through machines and new sources of power and energy. The separation of humanity from nature can be traced to the Age of Reason, during which René Descartes famously declared, "I think, therefore I am," giving the intellect a status it had never had before. The Cartesian split between the mind and body also reduced those who live in close contact with nature (most people in the world at that time) to primitive savages who needed to be conquered, controlled, and enslaved.

Judeo-Christian values, which would sweep the world through colonization, created this deep rupture between humanity and nature. Prior to monotheistic religions, many people the world over honored pantheons of gods, goddesses, and nature spirits. These religions were animistic, and nature was not seen as an object from which to extract the lumber and minerals we needed. Rather, plants, animals, rocks, the clouds, soil, and other natural objects were known to be infused with an animating spirit that allowed for a sacred relationship, or ayni. However, the god of the Old Testament insists that humans were made in "his" image (note the absence of a feminine counterpart, despite the fact that many cultures have associated nature with the Great Mother) and were given free rein to dominate Earth. This spirit of domination and conquest perpetuates the lie that humans are separate from nature—that we are superior—and creates the conditions for the exploitation of the natural world and the oppression of those who are perceived as being close to nature or less "civilized," including women and Indigenous people.

Although some might believe that being permanently at the top of the food chain is the best place to reside, this perpetuates the sense of separation and suffering. Deep within, we long to be cradled and nourished by our natural environment. Meanwhile, our souls recognize the truth of our interconnectedness with all beings and the need to collaborate in creating a healthy future world. When our egos choose to defy this foundational law of nature, we end up stuck behind the walls of protection, and we make an enemy out of our beautiful world. We lose our sense of deeper meaning, higher purpose, and sacredness. Out of the numbness of our alienated state, we grieve for something whose name we have forgotten.

We must remember that the waters are sacred, for they clean and nourish us—literally and figuratively. The Earth is sacred, for just like a loving mother, she feeds and nurtures us. The light of the sun is sacred, and we cannot continue filling the skies with so much smoke and pollutants from burning fuel. We also need the rich darkness of night and the gentle light of the moon, which is so crucial to our psyches and the regulation of our nervous systems. Instead, our city lights create perpetual light pollution, blocking our vision of the stars and our access to wonderment. Animals and insects often get lost too, especially when they are engendered to feel their way in the dark and the natural light of the night. Our circadian and natural rhythms, uninterrupted for ages, have been disrupted.

All these factors are, to a degree, the cause of anxiety and other mental disorders, which are rampant in today's world. A few friends who live in New York City have shared with me the number of conscious rituals (walks in the park, yoga, meditation, drinking green juices) they have to go through every day just to keep a baseline for their nervous system.

In order to cultivate our sense of wholeness—feeling light, inspired, and grounded at the same time—we have to return to a state of harmony with each of the elements. This includes the elements within our physical bodies; for instead of intellectualizing our communion with Spirit, we can realize its palpable manifestation.

Practice: Building Your Bands of Power

Overall, to feed the bands, it is helpful to spend time in nature and feel the elements in their purest expression: the earth beneath you, the waters flowing around you, the air breathing you, the light of the sun, and the ethereal presence of the Great Spirit who infuses everything in your surroundings. If you live close to nature, this is readily available; if you are in a city or suburb, you can visit a park or take a short trip to a place where the elements are more vibrant.

Once you find a place in nature, or at home by your altar (you can find instructions for how to summon the elements to your altar in the Appendix), find a comfortable place to sit and take a few breaths to relax and connect with yourself and your intention.* Begin by calling the earth element, imagining the most black and fertile soil. Allow it to form the first band around your body (usually four fingers wide) just below the belly, at the same level where most people wear belts. This band can also be like a disc adding an extra horizontal dimension. Take a moment to reflect on your deep longings and imagine you are sowing them in the form of seeds on this black earth.

Next, summon the water element and visualize it organizing a second band around your body at the solar plexus. Imagine it is red and that its temperature is perfect to bring you healing and purification. Allow the waters of this band to wave freely and to trickle like a rain over the black band to irrigate the seeds of your longings.

Immediately after, begin to summon the fire element to create a golden third band at the level of your chest. Allow its gentle warmth to nurture your heart and soften any emotional pains and fears. Keep feeling the warmth and allow it to radiate its light all the way to your belly to germinate the wet seeds of your deepest desires.

---

* If you have received the bands from a Munay-Ki practitioner and you have also learned how to feed the bands, then you can go through the process in this setting.

For the fourth band, begin to summon the air element like a gentle breeze that comes to liberate your throat and free your self-expression. Spend as much time as needed with this liberating wind. Then let this band settle in its silver color, which is connected to the light of the moon. Visualize this light shining over your growing seeds, and witness how each seed becomes the mature plant or tree that it is meant to be. Then imagine that your plants or trees bear fruit, which produce new seeds. Finally allow the wind of this band to spread those new seeds to fresh grounds, symbolic of your consciousness expanding as your longings manifest and sprout.

Until now, with the power of the elements and the blessing of each band, you have energetically activated your dreams. Yet, with the last band at the level of your forehead, you will purify your whole process of gestation and manifestation. Let the purest white light of the sun and stars form this fifth band like a disc or even a halo around your head. And allow this pristine vibration to expel any thoughts or energies that are toxic, heavy, or negative.

To further work the Bands of Power, make sure you receive the rite from a Munay-Ki practitioner and follow their instructions for activating the bands.

Chapter 3:

THE HARMONY RITE

Sometimes it is difficult for us to realize when we are losing our instincts, for it is often an insidious process that does not occur all in one day, but rather over a long period of time. Too, the loss or deadening of instinct is often entirely supported by the surrounding culture, and sometimes even by other women who endure the loss of instinct as a way of achieving belonging in a culture that keeps no nourishing habitat for the natural woman.

— CLARISSA PINKOLA ESTÉS, PH.D.,
WOMEN WHO RUN WITH THE WOLVES

The third Munay-Ki transmission is known as the Harmony Rite, or Ayni Karpay (*ayni* is the Quechua word for sacred reciprocity with the land and all our relations). Seven archetypes are installed along the spine in the position of each energetic center or chakra (which can be correlated with the Hindu chakra system). This transmission of seven archetypes enables us to walk through life with a greater sense of peace, power, wisdom, and harmony with all other beings.

What is an archetype? Carl Jung, who coined the term, believed that archetypes are powerful symbolic representations of energies that exist within the collective unconscious. The conscious realm is simply what we are already aware of (or what constitutes the terrain of "ordinary" reality), whereas the unconscious realm is far more expansive and contains all that remains largely hidden from us. Dreams, rituals, and trance states help us tap into both the personal and collective unconscious. The personal unconscious is the realm of our own private mythology, which is potentiated by our life experiences, particularly memories that our conscious mind has forgotten, repressed, or rejected. Within it lie both our personal shadow and our greatest medicine. The collective unconscious, in contrast, is not unique to individuals but constitutes what Jung called "psychic structures" that are shared across time in all cultures. It is also the place of the *numinous*, a term that refers to the great and inexpressible mystery—to the Divine itself.

You can think of the collective unconscious as the psychic ground of humankind, and of archetypes as the characters that populate this realm. Jung wrote, "From the unconscious there emanate determining influences . . . which, independently of tradition, guarantee in every single individual a similarity and even a sameness of experience, and also of the way it is represented imaginatively."* Such archetypes can include deities as well as immediately recognizable figures, such as the Mother, the Father, the Trickster, the Wise Woman, and a host of others. (For a tangible connection to archetypes, you can simply look at a tarot deck or characters in a fairy tale.)

While archetypes can appear in a symbolic form, it is important to understand that archetypes are not merely symbols. They are real powers that show up in our lives regardless of if we are aware of them or not. When we are in proper relationship with an archetype, it is medicine, but too much or too little can become dangerous for the soul—just like fire can warm or burn and ice can refresh or freeze.

In the Harmony Rite, we receive and befriend the energy of four animal spirits the people of the Andes and Amazon revere: serpent, jaguar, hummingbird, and eagle/condor. From their light side, these archetypes offer us everything from enriched vitality

* Jung, Carl. *The Collected Works of Carl Jung, Volume 9 (Part 1)*: "The Archetypes and the Collective Unconscious:" Bollingen Series XX. Princeton: Princeton University Press, 1969.

to enhanced vision. They help us reset and enhance our instincts so we can maintain physical and emotional health. Through their keen abilities of sight, sound, smell, and perception, they steer us away from danger and lead us to safety and nourishment. We all know what it is like to end up in the "wrong place at the wrong time," or with the "wrong people" because we didn't anticipate the consequences of our choices. However, these animal spirits enhance our tracking abilities by helping us perceive through their perspective, which helps us avoid toxic situations and choose a healthier path. For example, one of the serpent's gifts is to feel with its skin, so it might alert us by giving us goose bumps when danger lurks. The jaguar, on the other hand, is very visceral and may alert us to danger with a gurgling stomach.

By receiving constant input from these allies and honing our ability to communicate and perceive with and through them, we cultivate a better sense of what we need—of what is life-affirming and what is detrimental. This is crucial, as much of our so-called civilized world has wrested us from our full integrity as instinctive, animalistic beings. Because of the human propensity to place itself above nature, we in the Western world have negated or cruelly exploited the gifts of our animal brothers and sisters, rather than learning from them. As we work with the animal archetypes, our own instinctive nature improves over time. This occurs on several levels, from finding greater stability and confidence in every footstep to recognizing the opportunities life is offering us from a more expansive perspective.

Next, we receive three archangel-like archetypes that enable us to have a more fluid relationship with all aspects of our being, from dark to luminous. These Guardians are spiritual beings that are present in every culture; their expressions will be unique, depending on the time and place, but their essence is ultimately unchanging. The first one is the Guardian of the Underworld, the dark place of non-ordinary reality that is the fertile space for inner reflection, dream time, and is also the domain of the dead. The second is the Guardian of the Middle World, who presides over the worldly plane, including what we must do to live purposeful lives in ayni with all our relations. Finally, the Guardian of the Upper World connects us to the heavens, where we can access the light and more subtle parts of our being while gaining a vaster and more detailed perspective about the enlightened potential of our becoming.

Each of these "worlds" has its own set of qualities, and learning to navigate them gives us greater flexibility in responding to the changes and challenges of our lives as well as a broader awareness of the hidden spiritual influences that may be impacting us. The three worlds also correlate to the three times (past, present, and future), and they are always in dialogue with one another. If we look at time through a merely linear perspective, we will surmise that the future is the result of the present and the present is the result of the past. However, from a nonlinear shamanic perspective, the future can affect the present, and the present can affect the past. When we work with the Guardian archetypes, we develop further awareness about our subconscious (past), conscious (present), and superconscious (future), and we come to regularly discover deeper meaning and synchronicity in our daily lives. A familiar example of synchronicity (another one of Jung's terms) is the experience of "randomly" running into someone with whom we need to clear up a misunderstanding or disagreement or someone who gives us a necessary clue about the next step we need to take on our path.

ORIGINS OF THE HARMONY RITE: RECEIVING THE MEDICINE

When Alberto was exploring the jungle in his early 20s, he worked with master herbalists and researched many healing plants. During an encounter with a Huachipaire shaman, Don Alejandro Jahuanchi, Alberto conceived the idea for this Munay-Ki initiation. In a ceremony, Don Alejandro chanted the Eshuva songs, which are the prayers of the Huachipaire people that summon the healing spirits of nature. During this ceremony, the shaman transmits the powers of the jungle—such as the spirit of a particular bird or plant that will be of benefit to the person—by singing and blowing them into an energy center on the initiate's body.

While the Huachipaire shaman chanted to Alberto and blew into him forces of the jungle, including the jaguar and eagle, in later ceremonies Alberto received other archetypes. In the end, he chose to work with seven archetypes and incorporate them into the seven primary energy centers (chakras) for this rite.

Alberto understood that he needed to give residence to these forces within his energy body to intimately learn from them and work with them. Then he shared these archetypes with his students, confident that they could help bring peace, power, wisdom, and harmony to their lives.

Of all the Munay-Ki initiations, the Harmony Rite had the most vivid and immediate impact on my daily life as soon as I received it. Twenty years ago, when I was trying to figure out my future, I would summon these archetypes to help me perceive opportunities beyond my immediate fears and circumstances. In my first book, *Awakening Your Inner Shaman*, I shared how I journeyed through a sense of helplessness and hopelessness to a place of trust and certainty while in the embrace of these four animal totems.

Once we receive the archetypes, they remain with us and continue to impact our lives in mysterious ways, drawing us toward issues that need resolution so that we can experience harmony. Many years ago, Alberto and I were in India (a huge country with many cities and a virtually infinite number of streets and people); suddenly, walking toward Alberto in a straight line was a neighbor from California, with whom he had unresolved feelings. We were not attending any events that would have made such an encounter probable. Knowing that it was an extraordinary sign, Alberto and his neighbor met later in the day and cleared their lingering issues.

The consequences of working with these archetypes are unsurpassed and reveal to us the mysteries of our interconnectedness. They can help us clear the pain and confusion that may keep us bogged down in unhealthy patterns so that we can enter a more natural relationship with ourselves and the world around us.

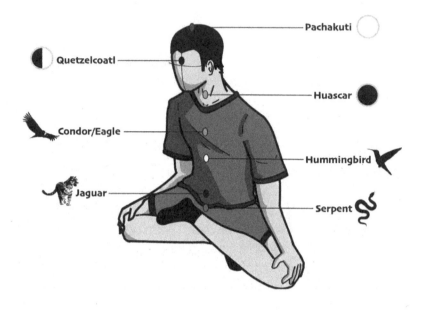

THE SEVEN ARCHETYPES

The Animal Spirits

There are four spirit animals that can be associated with the four major structures of the human brain: the reptilian brain, limbic brain, neocortex, and frontal lobes. These archetypes interact in important ways. For example, your serpent—associated with the self-preserving reptilian brain—might recognize the presence of hunger and the need to do something about it. Your jaguar—associated with the emotional limbic brain—might ensure that you find and eat your food, perhaps sharing it with those you love but hiding it from those who you perceive as "other." But then, the hummingbird—represented by the more altruistic neocortex—will make you look around, outside your intimate circle, to see if there is anyone else who needs to be fed. And the eagle/condor—with the spiritual view of the frontal lobes—might choose to relax, fast for the day, or wait until everyone is fed before deciding to eat.

This is what it means to engage our full intelligence, which is necessary for any great civilization to flourish. Altogether, the animal spirit archetypes encourage a more holistic vision and help you to examine forward and backward, to contextualize the events of the past so that you can project toward the future with greater clarity, intentionality, and foresight. The animal archetypes and the Guardians also represent the state of liminality, wherein one may exist between different worlds and be capable of navigating between seemingly opposing realities to gain insight and wisdom that would otherwise not be accessible. In this way, they encourage us to go beyond our limited perspectives and reach deeper, higher, and more complete truths.

Serpent

The serpent is associated with the physical body and our ancient reptilian brain connected to the autonomic nervous system, which regulates heart rate, breathing, the digestive system, body temperature, and sexual arousal, all of which are spontaneous, naturally occurring, physiological responses. This part of the human brain is also associated with the brain of early vertebrates. It predates the evolution of mammals, and its behaviors are concerned primarily with self-preservation.

The serpent is also closely connected with the root chakra, the energy center located at the base of the spine and at the perineum that correlates with the element of earth. When this chakra is clear and balanced, it grounds us into the earth itself, giving us a sense of safety, belonging, and rootedness. This becomes an important foundation from which to build all other aspects of our being.

The serpent perceives reality in a kinesthetic, tangible, and literal way. It is the force that keeps us breathing and digesting and helps us to maintain bodily integrity and health. With the help of this ally, we can learn to pay greater attention to the sensations of the body; in learning the body's language, which many of us have lost access to in our intellectually oriented societies, we can also develop a more comprehensive vocabulary for our experiences with nature—as we ourselves are nature.

Think of how a serpent slithers through life, highly aware of the texture of its path—whether it's soft or rough, dry or wet. When working with the serpent, we can become more attuned to what keeps our physical bodies in balance and our psyches out of harm. As an example, I might remember to take deep cleansing breaths more often, or I might feel an intuitive alarm signal in the form of a shiver up my spine when I am amid jealous or malicious energies.

Mythically, the serpent is associated with death because it moves so close to the ground, often hiding in concave and dark spaces, and because it sheds its worn-out skin as soon as it feels too tight, about 4 to 12 times a year. However, serpents are also associated with renewal, the creative life force, and fertility, as they slither out of their old skins, ready to welcome newness. Many wisdom traditions also associate the serpent with healing and immortality; the ancient Greeks believed that serpents were sacred to the god of medicine, Asclepius, who carried with him a staff with a snake curling around it—a symbol of his healing powers (which has also become the universal representation of Western medicine).

Perhaps, most of all, the serpent represents the capacity to make peace with paradox. When we are able to hold the dynamic tension of seeming opposites, we come to a sense of reconciliation that moves us beyond black-and-white thinking and facile dualities such as "good" and "evil." We reach a non-dual awareness that enables us to hold reality in all its perplexing and mind-bending contradictions. For example, the alchemical image of the ouroboros, the serpent eating its tail, articulates the notion that life is a continuum: birth leads to death, and death to life, over and over again. Neither is truly separate from the other but part of one smooth consecutive process of transformation.

Thus, the serpent can be a wonderful ally when it is time to let go of what no longer serves our evolution while allowing the new aspects of the self that will best support our life journey to freely develop. This applies to belief systems, behaviors, lifestyles, relationships, and any other aspect of our beingness.

Jaguar

The jaguar is associated with the emotional body and the limbic/mammalian brain that first appeared in small mammals about 150 million years ago. The limbic system interacts with other parts of the brain and impacts our emotions, moods, sensory processing, attention span, instincts, and motor control. It is associated with intense emotional charge, running the gamut from fear to rage to pleasure. Just like humans, jaguars have a sophisticated limbic system that supports emotions, perception of time, and long-term memory development.

The jaguar is also closely connected with the sacral chakra, the energy center located in the sacral region of the body (hips, low back, sexual organs) and correlated with the element of water. Its purpose is to bring greater emotional flow into our lives and encompasses pleasure, sensuality, creativity, and desire. Opening to pleasure helps us feel more joyful and expansive, and it helps us release energetic blockages around knowing who we are and what we want. One of the most important functions of jaguar medicine is to fully inhabit our lives with certainty and grace.

The perception associated with the jaguar is deeply visceral—instinctive and dealing with elemental, gut-level emotions. We all know the sensation when our head says "go there" but our belly says "don't." Or, perhaps we meet someone for the first time and they seem nice enough, but some deeper part of us warns us not to get too close to that person, or our sense of smell affirms to us that they can't be trusted. Overall, the jaguar offers us great protection, helping us to see what is hidden or to discern when someone is acting out of integrity.

When we work with the jaguar, we hone our natural instincts and learn to be agile and alert, even as we navigate our lives in a serene and unperturbed way—fully inhabiting the present moment. We come to feel more alive and limber, and we may be able to differentiate faraway sounds, discern smells, or know what's what in the dark, literally and figuratively. After all, jaguars perceive in the dark at least six times more than humans do, and jaguar medicine can do wonders when it comes to helping us see beyond superficial appearances.

Since jaguars have no predators in their wild environment, they can truly enjoy life. Many ancient myths and legends portray this great feline as the king of the jungle. The ease and pleasure with which the jaguar navigates its surroundings gives us the sense that we can also trust and delight in life. The jaguar can help us access deeper courage in facing difficulties and connect with our own inner ferocity, even if it has previously felt inaccessible, by greeting our emotions rather than fearing or repressing them.

With great stealth, jaguars can track their prey from a distance without being seen or heard. Then, without missing their mark, they spring upon it in one leap. Thus, our focus and certainty can be fortified by working with the jaguar, even in times of doubt and confusion. This can serve us well at every stage of our life. In Andean mythology, the jaguar is a spiritual guide that sees through death and knows how to leap out of this life alive—so it can be a powerful companion when it is time to cross the rainbow bridge, which connects us from this earthly realm to the realms that await us after death.

My experience of receiving the energy of this archetype occurred 20 years ago, when I first went to Peru with Alberto and the Four Winds Society. I had the chance to experience the work of an ayahuasca master, Don Ignacio Duri. Although he looked like a frail old man, in action he proved to be as sturdy as the local iron tree. This trip took place before my time in the mountains (which I mentioned in the Introduction of this book), and while I was very excited to be there, I didn't have any particular intentions, mostly because I did not know what to expect; after all, this was during an era before people became accustomed to conducting Internet research prior to a trip!

I found myself in a *maloca*, a ceremonial lodge, in the darkness of the night, without any lights. I felt the vibrations the old master created when he whistled and shook a *chacapa*, a bundle made with leaves. Some kaleidoscopic visions began to dance along with the rhythms, and then I felt an urge to urinate. Although I was quite wobbly, I made my way outside and down a set of stairs, pointing a small torchlight ahead of me. I relieved myself among bushes, the silver light of the moon shining bright on the moist foliage. Suddenly, with my pants still down, my gaze fell upon a pair of intense, fluorescent green eyes staring back at me. They were the eyes of a corpulent black jaguar that was only six or so feet away. I froze for a moment while my heart raced at a great speed. Right then, I recalled the words of an anthropologist I had met years earlier: "Come with me to the jungle and do ayahuasca. The spirit of the jaguar will come so close to you, you'll hear it breathe!"

I was fascinated and terrified, and then something even more incredible happened. Another pair of eyes appeared next to the first, and then another to the side, and then another—until a row of majestic black cats with fluorescent green eyes were standing in front of me.

My heart pounding, I managed to make my way back to my corner inside the maloca. Once seated, I looked around in the almost pitch blackness to try to form a sense of reality. Then, still in awe, I hid my head between my bent knees—and soon, all went black. However, just a few moments later, I sensed a presence calling for my attention, and I couldn't resist. What a surprise when I lifted my gaze and saw the black jaguar with vivid green eyes jumping through the window in full extension—front paws, head, neck, and the rest of its body all crossing the mosquito net. It happened so quickly, but it was almost as if I were seeing it in slow motion. The jaguar leaped and landed inside my body, entering through my head. Swiftly, it rearranged itself so its paws became my paws, its legs became my legs, and I suddenly had a furry, black tail. I intuitively stretched to let the jaguar in as our bodies merged in this magical way.

Now I was looking through its eyes, and my sight became sharper in the darkness and my body felt strong and supple. At some point, I sensed an urge to go outside again, so I did. I went for a little walk in the dark jungle, at times crouching to feel my four limbs on the earth. I had the extraordinary experience of walking in a jaguar's body, its heart beating both calm and strong. I was no longer afraid, as I knew nothing could harm me.

This is how I received the jaguar archetype—through the gift of a direct transmission from the spirit of the jungle and jaguar itself.

Hummingbird

The hummingbird is associated with the individual soul's journey through this lifetime and with the neocortex, a complex brain structure that commands our higher functions, including sensory perception and cognition. It is also the part of the brain associated with language as well as creative and artistic thinking and altruism.

The hummingbird correlates with the solar plexus chakra, the energy center that is located at the pit of the stomach and is associated with the element of fire and personal willpower. We access this power through a combination of clear intention and dedicated action, and it becomes a gateway to creative living. This is the space of mastery—and the hummingbird shows us that mastery comes from generating fruitful possibilities.

In its pursuit of flowers, colors, and nectar, the hummingbird inspires us to look for beauty and to create beauty around us. It helps us remember that which is sweet and easy about life—which is especially important in times when we are subject to depressive thinking or when we think of ourselves as nothing more than powerless victims. The hummingbird, which is all about swift movement and fresh energy, encourages us to lighten up. After all, we didn't come here to suffer and complain; we came here to find the nectar of life!

Working with this sacred totem, our instinct is reset so our focus becomes joy and levity rather than problems and conflict. With its swiftness, the hummingbird steers us away from reactive behaviors that might cause us to create more burdens and danger and helps us to perceive opportunities for harmony amid the most perilous crises.

With its ability to migrate hundreds of miles to find warmth, flowers, and nectar, this beautiful little bird accomplishes the impossible journey. As the smallest bird in the world, it does not stop to think, *My wings are too small*, or *There are no flowers to suck over the sea.* It simply migrates toward the abundance that it knows exists. In this way, the hummingbird invites us to transcend our excuses for why we cannot live our dreams: "My children are too young"; "My job wouldn't allow it"; "My husband needs me at home"; "I need more money." Rather, it invites us into a more creative and life-affirming way of being in the world. It encourages us to say yes to our own epic possibilities, to do what it takes to embody our calling and passion for life.

In Indigenous tribes across the Americas, the hummingbird is a sacred being that symbolizes vibrancy, vitality, ability, flexibility, speed, efficacy, and messages from the spirit realms. I had a clear experience of these years ago, when I was dealing with a conflict with one of my friends. Although I loved her dearly, she tended to push my boundaries frequently and to feel entitled to my time and space. I felt overwhelmed and disrespected, but I didn't know how to confront the situation. On one occasion, as I was pondering what to do, a hummingbird crashed into my window. I thought nothing of it at the time, and I certainly didn't imagine it was a message from the spiritual realms. (Sometimes, in the words of Sigmund Freud, a cigar is just a cigar!) However, the next day, another hummingbird crashed into my window, and I found that quite strange. Later that week, I stepped out of my car and found a dead hummingbird at my feet. With so many consecutive wounded hummingbirds, I realized that my own hummingbird archetype was attempting to make me more aware of my emotional porosity, sending me a message that my friend was overstepping my boundaries. I could feel that my incapacity to respond was debilitating to me and that my hummingbird had been taking the hit for me. At this point, grateful to my hummingbird, I found the courage to set my boundaries in this relationship so I would not have my life force sucked dry and would return to my vitality.

Eagle/Condor

The eagle/condor is associated with the part of us that is always connected to the Great Spirit. It corresponds to the frontal lobes, the part of the brain that is connected to higher-order thinking and our capacity to create meaning and follow a spiritual path. It is the most highly evolved region of the brain and represents our future potential as the new human, *Homo luminous*.

The eagle/condor is connected to the heart chakra, the energy center that allows us to feel unconditional love and includes an open-hearted, friendly, and noncoercive goodwill toward all. This kind of love transcends tribalistic ideas of "me" and "mine" and recognizes the interconnectedness of all beings. It is unmoored from selfish desires, but rather attuned to a higher perspective. The heart is the center point, where our earthly and heavenly qualities and potentials meet.

With their majestic flight, their preference to nest in high places, and their keen vision, eagles and condors maintain a vast and sharp perspective of the landscape below, reminding us to similarly look at our lives from a discerning distance. This broad view helps us to see around corners and to find unexpected ways around challenges we may be facing. These great winged ones continually invite us to soar to a higher vantage point.

In the Andes, condors are believed to be messengers between the worlds. And among many Indigenous groups of South America, eagles are similarly revered as spiritual intermediaries and intercessors, as they carry the souls of the deceased to the worlds beyond this one.

Why does this archetype combine the energies of eagle and condor, rather than selecting just one of them? I explain this in my book *Awakening Your Inner Shaman:*

> *In the shamanic lore of the Americas, a prophecy spoke about a time when the condor and the eagle would fly together, referring to the reunion between the sacred wisdom of the peoples of the North and the sacred wisdom of the peoples of the South. This gathering would revitalize the voice of the Earth, strengthen the peoples, and brighten the future.*

Nowadays, we recognize the fruits of these predictions as Indigenous people from all over the Americas gather to share their ways of communion, prayer, and offering.

Encountering either can be soul-stirring and life-changing. Years ago, while hiking in the Andes, my friend Monica went up a treacherous mountaintop and then couldn't figure out how to climb back down. Already initiated in the Munay-Ki Rites, she was awestruck when a condor flew right over to show her the best way down. Not once, not twice, but many times, the condor circled above to point Monica in the direction of the easiest wall. Following the condor's guidance, she made it to a safer gradient. At this point, she had run out of water and was feeling weak and thirsty. Again, the condor guided her to a little stream and remained with her until she made it to her base camp.

In the same way, we can ask the eagle or condor to show us the blessing when we only see challenges. From their view, there are no obstacles, only opportunities to soar higher and see with greater wisdom. They help us relax into our spiritual essence—as much as we are the earth and the other elements, we are also sublime and ethereal—and reset by contemplating the great expanse of the heavens. Also, when we grow too comfortable in a daily routine and begin to get stuck to the point of stagnation, the eagle and condor will nudge us out of the nest so we may spread our wings once again. With these great allies, we remember the transcendental aspect of life so we stop allowing ourselves to be overwhelmed by ordinary circumstances.

The Guardians

While the three Guardian archetypes can be correlated with a specific Indigenous character or deity, as you will read in the descriptions below, they are universal and therefore can be related to deities and figures from other religious and mythological pantheons. After all, there are multiple examples of gods or keepers of the underworld (Hecate, Skeleton Man, Kali), of the Middle World

(Seshat, Cernunnos, Pan), and of the Upper World (Nut, Masauwu, Odin) across different traditions. In working with any of the three Guardians, you may choose to associate them with archetypes from your own spiritual or cultural tradition. Each Guardian will acquire the personal costume that your psyche assigns to it, and it may even ask you to call it a name that is more familiar to you.

The Guardian of the Lower World

The keeper of the Lower World is an ally who can be greatly beneficial to us when we wish to facilitate an easier and more fluid relationship with our inner unconscious, which may require navigating buried memories, trauma, and any aspects of our own human shadow that we have disowned and must come to peace with. Since the origins of the Munay-Ki are in the Andes, we summon Huascar, who was the head of the mystery school during the time of the Inka Empire. According to lore, when he died at the hands of the Spaniards, betrayed by his brother, Inka Atahualpa, he took the wisdom teachings with him to the Lower World, ensuring that they would be safe from the conquest and the later Inquisition. Today, we know these teachings have resurfaced to help the world walk through times of great pain and difficulty. The Munay-Ki are an example of how the buried wisdom seeds are sprouting to offer hope and guidance.

This archetype corresponds to the throat chakra, which correlates with the element of wind. While the throat chakra represents your integrity and inner truth, and your capacity to convey it to others, many of us are taught to hide our deepest selves from view—particularly if we learned that it was unsafe to be who we are. However, when we reclaim these buried gifts, we experience greater harmony, self-expression, and authenticity. We bring the darkness to light.

The collective mind recognizes a dark landscape "down under" that is distinct from the one in which we normally reside. But while Judeo-Christian lore may classify this as "hell," ancient Indigenous traditions view the underworld differently. It is a mysterious place filled with forgotten memories and unresolved issues.

It is also a place inhabited by elemental forces capable of renewing the world. As we delve deeper into Earth, these elemental forces acquire such magnitude that no human being could venture there without being swallowed for eternity, for the underworld is so vast that we could easily become lost and terrified if we venture there with imprudence and without a guide. Lost souls and death lurk in all corners, and demons and hungry ghosts hide in every shadow.

If the underworld is so harrowing, why would anyone choose to venture there? In reality, we have no choice but to enter the depths in order to heal and to find redemption and wholeness. Eventually, the darkness begins to reveal its beauty and gems. Being a place of transformation, magnificent gifts abound. Certain emotional states, dreams, and crises demand that we go into different levels of the depths to surrender and come out on the other side, restored. The archetypal hero's or heroine's journey portrays the full experience and tells us about the hidden treasures waiting for those who are courageous enough to embark on the quest.

A wonderful example of this is the Sumerian myth of the descent of Inanna, known as the Queen of Heaven and Earth, into the underworld. She is sundered to pieces by her shadow sister, Ereshkigal, but she eventually returns to the surface; having died, she is reborn. Inanna, like others who dared to go where few people willingly go, understood what the mystics of ancient times knew: some of the most precious gems of humanity are hidden in the depths of the Lower World.

It's a good idea to call on Huascar when it is important to reconnect with aspects of our lives that are submerged in the subconscious. We can ask Huascar to aid us in understanding and remembering our dreams and guide us through the night or darker emotional and mental terrains. Huascar is also a great guide for shamanic journeywork, whereby medicine people can help to retrieve soul fragments that have gotten stuck in the Lower World. He can lead us to our wounding so we may shine our light on those places crying for our attention and go through the process of integration.

The Guardian of the Middle World

The Guardian of the Middle World can help us manifest exactly what will help us heal the past so we can claim an auspicious destiny. In the Munay-Ki path, this Guardian is represented by Quetzalcoatl, the feathered serpent, also known to the Aztec as the Lord of the Dawn, the Day Bringer, the Morning Star. According to legend, he was banished after being betrayed by the Smoking Mirror god. Before disappearing in the ocean, he promised he would return. In fact, central to Quetzalcoatl's story is the notion of return.

The Quetzal is a beautiful jungle bird from Central America. *Coatl* means "serpent" in the Aztec language of Nahuatl. This feathered serpent, a potent symbol of the connection to the earthly and heavenly realms, brought irrigation, medicine, stonework, music, and dance to humanity. For the Mayans, he was Kukulkan. Like him is the goddesses Isis, who brought wisdom, the arts, and agriculture to the human world.

This archetype corresponds to the third-eye chakra, which correlates with the element of light. Each chakra has an important spiritual component, but this center in particular opens us up to our visionary capacities—associated with the power of the imagination, which connects us to both material and spiritual dimensions, revealing wisdom to live with greater purpose. It is the chakra of the Aquarian Age, in which ideas can gain currency, and dreams can become reality in an instant. It also connects us to a luminous dimension in which the light of all the worlds comes to bear upon this present moment. Time and space can be transcended, and we have the ability to usher in new paradigms and to directly perceive what may have been hidden or unknown, either in the depths of earth or the wide expanses of space.

The Middle World is the vivid dimension of everyday life in the place of here and the time of now. The Guardian of this realm is the archetypal presence that can manifest auspicious synchronicities for us, from finding a perfect parking spot on a busy day, to bumping into the right person who helps direct us to the job of our dreams, to arriving just in time to witness the last sacred breath of a loved one. In other words, this Guardian can synchronize the past and future to generate meaningful circumstances in the present moment. It is the aspect of consciousness that is aware of our destiny and of our yesterday.

We can call on Quetzalcoatl to help us be in harmony—right relationship—with reality so we don't have to micromanage our lives. Instead, we can enter into a sacred flow with the river of life. We have all experienced that magic before, and with the help of this Guardian, we can magnify that magic in our daily lives. Suddenly, we find ourselves in the right place at the right time, more often than not, manifesting realities we may not have previously imagined. Of course, every possibility contains its shadow, so this experience can sometimes feel like being in the wrong place at the wrong time. However, in the end, as we perceive through a higher spiritual vision, we see that at every moment we are exactly where we need to be according to the state of our being—not separated from the rest of humanity and all creation—and the evolutionary lessons that need to be mastered.

The first time I understood this archetype in my own body, I was working with a group of women at our retreat center in Chile. We had spent the whole week in ceremony with the elements—we walked a spiral to connect with the depths of the earth, we purified ourselves in herbal baths, and we chanted inside a sweat lodge resembling the womb of the Great Mother. Everything felt very earthy—a full immersion into our connection with Pachamama. At the end of our journey together, we went on a vision quest, hiking up a mountain to cross over a pass. Many women there had received the Munay-Ki Rites and had the archetype of Quetzalcoatl within them. Like me, some of these women felt their serpent acquiring wings as we climbed. The farther we went, the more our wings grew. It was Quetzalcoatl—a beautifully tangible experience of being completely grounded and up in the air at the same time. We'd been immersed in serpent energy, with our bellies close to the earth, and now, our wings were growing and expanding, with the spaciousness and vision that come from the eagle and our connection to the Upper World. By the time we reached the top of the mountain, some of us were fully experiencing Quetzalcoatl, who acts as a divine conduit between Earth and Heaven, allowing us to engage with the intimate details of our lives and the bigger picture at the same time.

The Guardian of the Upper World

The ninth Inka ruler, Pachakutec is the mythic Guardian of the Upper World. Stepping outside of linear time, he is capable of bringing about heavenly order. Coming into a conscious relationship with Pachakutec allows us to recognize and embrace our destiny. He guards the entry veils to the Upper World—to our ultimate becoming, to all possibilities for ourselves and humanity. He not only opens the gates for us to journey and connect with our destinies but also guides and helps us as we make that quest. During Pachakutec's rule, the Inka Empire dramatically expanded from the valley of Cusco to include nearly all western South America. It was also during his rule that Machu Picchu came to be; most archaeologists believe it was built as one of his estates. Pachakutec was a great visionary, and as such, he can show us where in the Upper World the possibilities for our own destiny exist.

This archetype corresponds to the crown chakra, which correlates with the element of consciousness. This is the seat of heavenly grace, awakening to the pure nature of reality, and connection to the great powers of the subtle dimensions.

The Upper World is the realm of heaven and of our cosmic origins—we transcend physical reality and recognize that existence is an infinite field of consciousness made up of energy and information. Universal consciousness itself is a hologram, which means that the entirety of the cosmos exists in even the smallest particle. From this awareness, we recognize that we are truly made of starlight. Here, we can orient ourselves to wholeness and the source of all creativity. We are able to empty ourselves out so that our egoic identities do not hinder us in any way. We become what the shamans call a hollow bone, in that we are clear conduits for higher consciousness.

When Pachakutec opens the gates to the Upper World, we can ask him to guide us to our most auspicious destiny so that we can start sourcing from there rather than merely living the results of our past karma and our genetic inheritance. With his help, we can dream the world into being by connecting to what's possible in our destiny lines, no matter how improbable it may seem. Often, destiny *is* improbable—possible, but improbable all the same. With this archetype, our previous perspectives are dwarfed by an ethereal vastness that guides us to a higher knowledge of reality. Life can make invisible leaps in our favor when we are connected to Pachakutec.

Throughout our world, we have seen the disastrous results of clinging to old ways of thinking about and doing things, even when they do not serve us . . . or the planet. With Pachakutek's help, we can learn to cede control and release the ways of the past—of brutalization, oppression, and disconnection from Earth and one another. Of course, getting to a new era requires navigating extreme tumult, including environmental degradation and various forms of social and political discord, and to actively participate in creating balance and harmony. Connecting with the keeper of the Upper World jump-starts our evolution and helps us to transform so that we can adopt the behaviors and perspectives that are necessary to living more sustainably.

When you seek guidance for the future, particularly if you feel helpless in these times of turmoil, Pachakutec steers you in the direction of positive change and allows you to glimpse the light of a new humanity. In this way, you will move toward not who you once were or who you think you are now but toward the best version of who you are becoming.

CONNECTING WITH THE ARCHETYPES

Much of what exists in wisdom traditions around the world comes from a direct connection to the powers that lie within the collective unconscious. Since time immemorial, people have dreamed of and experienced visions coming from the most powerful archetypes: thunder, dragons, volcano eruptions, ocean waves, and more. As it appears to the psyche, an archetype can assume sublime proportions, but it is a mistake to see it as merely the result of an active imagination. As Jung explained, "Archetypes were, and still are, living psychic forces that demand to be taken seriously, and they have a strange way of making sure of their effect. Always they were the bringers of protection and salvation, and their violation has as its consequence the 'perils of the soul' known to us from the psychology of primitives."*

Remember, the seven archetypes of the Harmony Rite are living psychic forces that serve to awaken or enhance qualities we already possess in our human potential. If you receive the transmission, the giver (a shaman or Munay-Ki practitioner) is enhancing the possibility of your relationship with this archetype, but it is up to you to take a step closer and accept the invitation to let the archetype work its magic directly in your life.

In general, when an initiate receives the Harmony Rite, they receive the medicine of all the archetypes at once in the form of seeds. However, sometimes the Munay-Ki practitioner will emphasize an archetype that is specifically relevant to the initiate and the medicine they require. Perhaps your body is weak from illness, but working with the jaguar over a longer time will give you the courage to view your situation with a newfound strength. Or maybe your life feels devoid of sweetness, which may prompt you to work with the hummingbird to integrate more beauty. It can be a beautifully rewarding experience to come to an understanding of how each archetype perceives reality; instead of being overwhelmed by the archetype's vastly different way of seeing things, one can come to know it gradually and through intentional relationship and dialogue.

Experienced medicine people or shamans may also choose to give not only the seed of the archetype but also the full-blown archetype to an initiate. Once, Alberto had a student named Jillian, an Olympic skier from the United States who was preparing for the World Cup. She was physically and psychologically very fit and strong, so Alberto felt confident that she could handle the spirit of the jaguar in its full form. In a sacred space, he gave Jillian this great feline and taught her to work with it. A few days later,

---

*   Jung, Carl. *The Collected Works of C.G. Jung, Volume 9 (Part 1)*. Princeton: Princeton University Press, 1969.

he did the same with the hummingbird, and a few days after that, with the eagle. Jillian worked to cultivate her relationship with the animal spirits, and soon after, she won the World Cup in Japan in the freestyle women's moguls event.

When I spoke with her a few months later, she explained, "When I am preparing to go down the race, I let jaguar embody me to enhance my stability, and I stay with jaguar as the race begins and I am descending the moguls. Once I am approaching the jump, I summon hummingbird to give me lightness and prepare me for the air. Then, I change to eagle to reach maximum flight and freedom while performing my aerials. To land, I call jaguar again, and I land in my 'four feet,' strong and balanced. . . . That is how I won Japan!"

While it is possible to maintain a lifelong robust relationship with the archetypes, under stress or crisis they can become weak or injured. I once experienced a very difficult physical situation with a lung infection due to mold. The illness took a huge toll on my body, so after a year I told Alberto, "Let's check on my serpent. I bet she's tired from putting up with all this coughing." Because the serpent is connected to our physicality and the autonomic nervous system—and is always helping us care for our physical health—I could sense that she was under duress. Sure enough, I discovered that she was exhausted. We sent her to the spirit world, and then we brought in a new manifestation of it. For months, this new serpent had me drinking a cup of chamomile tea (which I used to not like) and sent me to bed early at night, ensuring that my physical self was well tended.

In general, daily contemplation and actionable steps toward acknowledging and honoring the archetypes can help them to exist as constant self-renewing energies that remind us of our unbroken connection to them, as my colleague Martha shares in her story below:

> When I received the Munay-Ki, I was a yogi and a runner. To develop my relationship with each of the archetypes of the Harmony Rite, I would connect with them at the end of each run. When I stopped moving, my mind was calm and open, my body both relaxed and energized, and I

had a sense of oneness with all things and the feeling that anything was possible—a perfect environment for growing my seeds.

When all the chakras are balanced and the archetypes that reside within them are acknowledged and content, we feel at peace. We are both confident and humble as we move through the world. There is nothing to prove. No hiding, no grandstanding. One takes one's place in nature with a sense of purpose and gratitude.

They say that when you drive a supertanker and make a minute change in your steering, three months down the road, you see that you have navigated to an entirely different continent than you set out for. That's how I see the result of this energy work in my life. It's so subtle that I don't notice it until I look back and see an immense shift in my life.

EXPANDING OUR INTELLIGENCE TO INCLUDE OUR INSTINCTS

The seven archetypes of the Harmony Rite help us maintain the integrity of our whole beings. The three Guardian archetypes help us source from our becoming while illuminating our past, and the animal archetypes help us remain completely present in a healthy way. This gives us a grounded and holistic awareness that makes it easier to practice the sacred principle of ayni, which is woven throughout the daily lives and ceremonies of the Andean peoples. When we are in reciprocity with life, there is an auspicious balance between the expansive and the receptive energies within and around us—between giving and receiving. This initiation enables us to expand our intelligence so that it includes all aspects of our being, from the gift of our more material and embodied senses to that of our more subtle awareness.

Nowadays in modern culture, our instinct works in a flawed way because we have been impacted by limiting belief systems as well as personal and collective traumas that have impaired our capacity to know our wholeness and to perceive reality as it is. If we have not healed past traumatic or painful experiences, then we continue to see through the eyes of trauma. Some wisdom traditions within Indigenous cultures that experienced great trauma and loss hold powerful keys that enable us to self-resurrect. The archetypes that are associated with this rite are primordial forces that steward this process in that they enable us to perceive reality through their eyes, their bodies, their perceptual systems. They aid us in relating to the world in a way that is not our default but is more comprehensive.

Indigenous people preserving their traditional ways, and united in their breath and with nature, can feel and know when their prey is coming; they can hear the birds and predict when the rain will come. They are connected to the ecosphere and can track their food by simply maintaining a sense of acute presence with all their senses. In contrast, in the Western world, our intelligence is often focused only on seeing: social media, computers, television, external appearances. We forget to smell, we forget to hear, we forget to taste—and this is an immense loss, because each sense brings us so much information. We have lost the ability to track, to feel, to elicit information with our other senses. Rewilding— returning to our wild nature—offers us an intrinsic way to perceive reality. We come to reclaim our animal selves instead of seeing ourselves as superior or separate from the rest of nature, and we also recognize our attunement to realms that transcend the material. With a greater appreciation for the full picture of who we are, we come to embrace the underlying unifying essence that runs through all life.

Practice: Invite the Seven Archetypes into Your Life

Altogether, the seven archetypes constitute an ancient wisdom that lives in the collective unconscious of humanity, and although they are universal, they acquire specific colors and details depending on the culture and setting of the person who receives them. For instance, for one person, the serpent might appear as a boa constrictor, and for another person a cobra, and for another the mythic serpent of the Kundalini. Each of us has a unique way of relating to an archetype, depending on our own cultural practices and the symbols, myths, and stories that have impacted each one of us individually.

Knowing this, spend a week exploring and honoring your connection to each of the archetypes. You may discover a greater affinity to one or more of the archetypes; if this is the case, feel free to come back to and work with that archetype after you have explored all seven. For the purpose of this exercise, I suggest spending equal time with each archetype, as all of them are meant to be engaged with so that you can hone your instincts in a more holistic and well-rounded way.

You can work with the archetypes in order: serpent, jaguar, hummingbird, eagle/condor, the Guardian of the Lower World, the Guardian of the Middle World, and the Guardian of the Upper World. For ease, choose one day a week to connect with a new archetype—for example, every Sunday. On that specific day, light a candle on your altar or meditate somewhere peaceful in nature. Summon the presence of that archetype in your life and ask it to be your close teacher for the next week.

For the animal archetypes, it's useful to wake up every morning as if you were that archetype and to set the intention for that archetype to guide you. After all, each animal already exists in the various parts of the human brain. As you meditate on the archetype, you may wish to ask such questions as, "What should I eat? What should my recreational activities be? How can I best relate to people and the world around me? What guidance do you have for me in taking care of my physical, mental, and spiritual health? How can I best embody you?" You may also have other questions that are relevant to specific situations in your life. Notice any instinctive feelings or responses that arise in your body and mind as you ask the questions. What is the archetype activating inside you?

In contemplating the answers that come to you throughout each day, you may discover that a week of embodying serpent will help you to be more cognizant of your skin, your digestion, and the time spent under the warmth of the sun. And maybe a week of embodying jaguar will inspire you to practice greater emotional honesty with yourself and to trust your gut. With hummingbird, you may be prompted to see the world with a greater sense of levity. And with eagle/condor, perhaps you find yourself viewing your life from a higher perspective so that you don't get "hooked" by normally triggering events.

The Guardian archetypes are more connected to the exploration of your awareness, so the questions you choose to ask them may be less about your body and daily activities and more about your overall consciousness. When you engage with each archetype every morning, you may wish to practice automatic writing, a technique in which you write down a question you have. Then, without thinking through your response, you write whatever comes to mind, not pausing your pen on the paper or stopping to "edit" yourself. This is a powerful form of divination that allows us to access the deeper parts of our consciousness and seemingly find answers that come out of nowhere. Many people who have practiced automatic writing have written entire books channeled through the spirit realm. Some of the questions you may choose to ask the Guardian archetypes might include: "What are your gifts and qualities? How can these gifts and qualities be of service to me in my life?"

You may discover that the Guardian of the Lower World helps you to excavate old fears and to move more gracefully through the unknown and unstudied parts of your subconscious mind; answers may even crop up in your dreams. The Guardian of the Middle World may appear to you in the form of synchronicities that help you to be more confident in fulfilling your purpose. And the Guardian of the Upper World can connect you to a more unitive consciousness and give you powerful glimpses into your personal future as well as the future of our world.

Chapter 4:

THE SEER RITE

There is no need to remind the reader that the shaman is he who
"sees," because he is endowed with a supernatural vision. He sees
just as far into space as into time. Likewise he can perceive what
is invisible to the layman—spirits, gods, the soul. When he is being
initiated the future shaman is fed with crystals of quartz. In other
words, his capacity as a visionary, as well as his "science," comes to
him, at least in part, from a mystic solidarity with heaven.

— MIRCEA ELIADE, *THE FORGE AND THE CRUCIBLE:*
THE ORIGINS AND STRUCTURE OF ALCHEMY

And now we come to the Seer Rite, or the Kawak Karpay (*kawak*
is the Quechua word for "seer"), which enables the initiate to see
from a broader perspective. Whereas the Harmony Rite expanded
the initiate's capacity to perceive from multiple vantage points,
the Seer Rite equips us with a more immediate clarity in the present moment. It enables us to vividly discern the colors, textures,
etheric imprints, and elemental tendrils that are right here, hidden in plain sight. The Seer Rite expands our attunement to the
subtle realm of energy, but it goes beyond visual discernment by
connecting us to an internal knowing that is not separated from
the warmth of the heart. The Munay-Ki Seer perceives from the
eyes of the heart, with deep compassion and love.

A common question I receive from new students is, "How
can I begin to see the energetic realm that lives beyond ordinary

reality?" The answer is simple, but not easy. You must be willing to see not only what feels good and what you perceive as pleasant but also what might seem ugly or feel painful—what makes you feel shame, guilt, fear, or anger.

As we welcome our existence, exactly as we are, and stop pushing out of sight what is hurtful to us, we clear the filters of our vision. When we begin to accept reality as it is, beyond our preferences and limited ideas of "right" and "wrong," "fair" and "unfair," we start opening our "inner" eye (the third eye of the chakra system) and attuning to the more subtle dimensions. When we avoid paying attention to the uncomfortable aspects of our lives, we narrow the lenses through which we perceive. Instead of seeing the whole spectrum, we see only through the perspective of the ego—what the conscious mind gives permission to see. But if we can open to the possibility of illuminating what has remained in the shadows, our view expands to include the hidden facets of our being and our surroundings.

If keen discernment and an inclusive vision are necessary for our evolution, we must gather the courage and wisdom to look directly at our own shadow—and give ourselves the opportunity to uncover our woundings. For this reason, the Munay-Ki Rites are most effective as one body of wisdom rather than as isolated initiations; together, they give us a powerful technology for being guided toward our own hearts and wholeness.

When we receive the Seer Rite in particular, we receive luminous pathways that in turn activate new neural connections, allowing us to perceive in a more holistic way. As the image below describes, these pathways resemble a crown and a necklace. The crown describes the pathways that emerge between the third eye and visual cortex, which connects us to a more tangible awareness of the subtle dimensions. The shaman lays radiant lines diagonally and on both sides of the head, balancing the masculine and feminine, the golden and silver aspects of ourselves. With this beautiful crown of light, we expand our perspective beyond what we'd imagined possible into a cosmic vision of past, present, and future.

Then, for the vision to remain warm and compassionate, the shaman anchors this crown into the initiate's heart center with a luminous necklace so the vision is not cold and literal but infused with feeling and our own humanity. Connecting the heart to the visual cortex allows the initiate to see from the eyes of the heart.

As is true with all the Munay-Ki Rites, after receiving the initiation, it's auspicious to reinvigorate it until it feels well etched into your energetic body. For example, tapping on the third eye and all the pathways designated in the diagram, from the visual cortex to the heart, can reinforce the power of the transmission. In his book *Organization of Behavior: A Neuropsychological Theory,* published in 1949, neuropsychologist Donald Hebb described how pathways in the brain are formed and reinforced through repetition.[*] Later his theory was summarized by others as the metaphor "Neurons that fire together, wire together."

---

[*] Hebb, Donald. *The Organization of Behavior.* New York: John Wiley & Sons, Inc., 1949.

ORIGINS OF THE SEER RITE: AWAKENING THE SPIRITUAL EYE

In many shamanic traditions, secret technologies awaken the spiritual vision, and in the Munay-Ki, this is the Seer Rite, a transmission that Alberto brought from his work with the shamans from the coasts and jungles of Peru.

The medicine people from the coast are renowned for their ability to perceive beyond ordinary reality. In Quechua, they are known as the *kawak*—the individual who sees the spaces in between things and who has awareness of the invisible world in nature. A kawak can sense a person's energy field and diagnose their condition, or they may read your past and foretell your destiny.

The practices Alberto learned from the coastal peoples are still in use by the descendants of ancient cultures like the Chimu and Moche peoples.

One of Alberto's mentors from the northern coast, Don Eduardo Calderón, had an impressive altar, including amulets, interesting stones, swords, and power staffs, that allowed him to connect and dialogue with the invisible world and his spirit allies. He was a warrior of light, and his sight was so keen that he could diagnose disease by scanning his patients' energy fields. Don Eduardo would boast to Alberto that he could even tell him who his grandmother had slept with, in case he ever had any doubt about this paternal line!

Alberto also spent time studying in Cahuachi, in the southern coast. The monolithic figures in the Nazca plains depict a series of archetypes that ancient peoples etched into the arid desert more than 2,000 years ago. In these figures, you find enormous (more than 300 feet tall) images of a monkey with an extraordinary spiral-shaped tail, a spider, a hummingbird, and many other animals and geometric forms. The Nazca shamans must have been able to perceive beyond their smaller, village lives into the invisible realm of archetypes. Since these images can only be appreciated from above a certain height (tourists often hire small planes), Alberto believes that they may have been ways of exchanging messages with the heavens. There, Alberto learned that what we perceive with our ordinary senses, including our eyesight, is probably only a thin slice of a multidimensional reality that can be perceived by those who awaken their inner sight of the Kawak.

Before reaching the Colca Canyon, a dramatic valley with views of towering volcanoes, visitors can see pictographs etched into hundreds of rocks. These pictographs depict otherworldly beings with antennae, suggesting that the people of this land were attuned to a cosmic vision of the Universe that transcended Earth and extended into the vast reaches of space.

SEEING WHAT WE BELIEVE

Years ago, while leading an expedition to work with medicine plants in the Peruvian jungle, I met three new students who worked for the fashion industry. One of them was a fashion show producer, another was a clothing designer, and the third was a model. Every morning, while at breakfast in our eco lodge, I was mesmerized by the stupendous outfits they displayed; they were totally chic but completely useless for protection against mosquitoes and the relentless sun.

On our walkabouts, they proceeded carefully so as not to get scratched or bitten on their naked arms, backs, or legs. In the meantime, our local guide would spot all kinds of animals, insects, and creatures along the narrow path through the thick forest. He could see a small brownish frog from 15 feet away, although from the distance it looked like a rotting leaf among many others. He could also predict the exact minute when monkeys would come leaping across the canopy of trees. These were skills that eluded my new students and the rest of us, who were mesmerized by what we saw.

I became friends with these three ladies, and when they took me shopping in Manhattan, I was equally amazed by their tracking abilities. They could smell a dress from a favorite designer on sale in their exact size three blocks away, and they found gorgeous outfits for me in places I would have never thought of looking. I became sure that our jungle guide could never accomplish this level of precise differentiation in the concrete jungles of Manhattan, just as my new friends would never be able to identify and perceive such an array of life forms in the wild Amazonian rainforest.

This experience clearly portrays how we are conditioned to perceive according to the way we were taught to see reality—by our family, society, and culture—and in order to adapt to our environment. We also see through the lens of our individual psychic makeup and temperament. Even if we grew up with siblings under the same roof, we still develop a unique vantage point tinted by personal emotions and beliefs. For example, if I feel insecure, I'll be looking for protection; if I think I am unworthy, then I'll unconsciously find situations that prove it. In other words, our eyes will see what we believe.

The idea that we see what we believe was shown to me years ago when I visited Master Chén, a woman from China who lives in the United States and is considered a national treasure in her home country due to her reputation as an extraordinary seer and healer. Unfortunately, her early experiences as a healer were traumatic. Although many people from far and wide came to her village after learning about her marvelous abilities, rumors that she was a witch spread into the governing sector. She was publicly shamed, and the experience was so depressing that she nearly killed herself. She ended up in the hospital after suffering from severe burns that occurred when she attempted to set herself on fire. At the hospital, she had visions of various spirits who affirmed her healing powers and informed her about a knowledgeable woman in the forest, not far from Master Chén's home, who could help the young girl to further develop her gifts. After leaving the hospital, she found the woman in the forest and immersed herself in nature and the teachings from her mentor. From there, Master Chén developed an exceptional relationship with the spirit world, to the extent that she literally receives all kinds of herbal medicines from an invisible dimension to give to her patients.

I had the fortune to dream about the otherworldly place from which Master Chén obtains these medicines and to see how this exchange occurs. In my dream, I visited a mystical silent forest in a pristine, snowy landscape, and eventually I arrived at a yurt. Inside, an ancient-looking man toasted fragrant herbs while turning a prayer wheel and quietly murmuring unintelligible words. Looking on attentively and sitting near him was a boy with a peaceful semblance. I woke up from the dream at this point.

Master Chén confirmed that my dream revealed the venerable spirit healer preparing the herbs and the young boy who would then deliver the medicine. In my eyes and the eyes of the few friends I invited to experience her healings, everything happened with crystalline transparency. Master Chén would repeat a few mantras and mudras until a little compact ball of dried herbs would land in her hands as if a portal had opened up about 10 inches above in thin air. Then, she would give it to the person in the audience for whom it was intended. She did not wear long sleeves, bracelets, rings, or anything that could serve to block the view from her empty hands, as she wanted people to clearly see the medicine materializing seemingly out of nowhere.

I have been a firsthand witness to Master Chén's gifts and her miraculous healings, although healing doesn't always mean a physical cure. I had friend who was affected by an aggressive cancer and quickly ended up transitioning from this earthly plane—but through his sessions with Master Chén, he died without fear, in a clear state of luminosity and freedom from any attachments to the material world.

Over the years, I introduced Master Chén to many people I knew, desiring to bring them hope and healing for their own personal suffering. On one occasion, a good friend of mine took her husband to experience the extraordinary phenomenon of Master Chén's work. He is a renowned doctor with many credentials, and at the end of the session, he commented, "That is the best magic trick I have ever seen. But the fact that I cannot explain it doesn't mean it is true." He refused to believe what he had witnessed with his own eyes. His belief system was strongly rooted in reductionistic science, and he chose to deny this event rather than question his ideology.

While it is healthy to be skeptical, it is also true that our materialistic era discourages any openness to the possibility of other dimensions that are not easily explainable by existing scientific paradigms. To our detriment, we have collectively turned our curiosity away from the energetic world and are overly focused on physical realities that can be validated by our five senses. In fact, studies have revealed that while many people have reported experiencing mysterious phenomena that could be viewed as supernatural, they are likely to completely forget or filter out these moments in the absence of a paradigm that entertains the possibility of strange occurrences; this happens because the "strangeness" clashes with their prevailing belief systems. Our experience of reality is literally filtered by our beliefs.

On top of all these factors that work to alter our perception, our physiological needs can make us unreliable narrators of our reality. If we are hungry, our bellies and brains are going to be on the lookout for food and will ignore most anything that falls outside this survival instinct. Physiologically, we have tunnel vision and are not built or trained to see all layers of reality at the same time. Typically, our views are narrowed to what our ego determines to be a priority.

The way we have been trained to perceive impacts the stories we've told ourselves about the nature of reality. Whether we created our stories or someone created them for us, we have come to confuse them for reality. The characters in our stories take on a life of their own and come to dominate our lives. We might strive to understand and negotiate with these ravenous beings because we believe they are genuine—to the extent that we mistake them for our authentic self. However, their complaints, demands, and thirst for attention are endless; they keep us trapped in the monkey mind of constant rumination. We continue to be bombarded by the shrill voices of all those we've wronged or been wronged by. And they never shut up.

As we begin to master this insight, we start to see beyond the most simplistic, literal layers of reality. We begin to recognize the events from our early life that shaped and molded us and how our family, society, and culture have affected the person we've become. With this recognition, we can outgrow our old stories (about what is and isn't possible, about what is and isn't real, about who we are or aren't) and learn to craft ones that are not only better suited to whatever stage of our evolution we are in but also encompass a reality beyond our limited vision. Life will no longer imitate a carefully scripted and edited movie, and we'll begin to laugh at the artifice of our literal world. We will see that the emperor has no clothes, and never did.

SEEING BEYOND PROJECTIONS

A word of caution: no matter how much we come to be able to perceive the visible and invisible aspects of reality, I cannot emphasize enough how crucial it is to consider the idea of projections. To understand projections, we must understand the shadow. This is a psychological term that refers to the traits of our personality we have difficulty acknowledging as ours. These aspects literally remain hidden from our awareness because it's too painful or disgraceful to admit they are ours, so we deny they exist within us. The shadow also contains the magnificent attributes we may have—our beauty, our goodness, our shining talents—but feel shameful or unworthy to embody. Either way, we suppress these aspects from our conscious awareness, which can lead to difficult situations where we prefer to point the finger at others rather than take responsibility. This is how we end up projecting onto others what truly belongs to us in the first place.

Jung, noting the dangers of *projection*, said: "The pervasive defense mechanism known as projection is how most people deny their shadow, unconsciously casting it onto others so as to avoid confronting it in oneself. Such projection of the shadow is engaged in not only by individuals but groups, cults, religions, and entire countries, and commonly occurs during wars and other contentious conflicts in which the outsider, enemy or adversary is made a scapegoat, dehumanized, and demonized."

The Seer Rite encourages us to see not only the nice and pleasant but also everything that demands our attention in order to keep healing our wounds, shortcomings, and limitations.

It invites us to examine our projections, making an effort to recognize and understand our own triggers when we feel judgmental or reactive toward others or the world in general.

As I mentioned in the beginning of this chapter, if we cultivate the intention to see reality with naked eyes, even if it hurts, we'll start to see the many layers that comprise our existence. This means that we eventually move beyond our individual pain and shame and recognize the opportunities that are heralded by our most intense and difficult feelings. We start to see where the pattern of the projection began—possibly, before we were even born, with one or more of our ancestors. Moreover, we recognize the ramifications of our willingness to move in a healing direction, which each of the Munay-Ki Rites can support.

In order to fully take in the Seer Rite, we must be willing to take back our projections. We can do this through a thorough, step-by-step inquiry that begins by noticing when and why we get triggered. For example, perhaps our relationships with close friends and partners are characterized by a near-irrational jealousy. When was the last time we felt this way, and why? Can we trace the pattern back to its first occurrence?

Our triggers are less about the present moment than they are about patterns we've been carrying for a long time and are associated with early wounds that caused us to internalize limiting beliefs about ourselves and the world. We can recognize our triggers whenever we feel a strong emotion about something that causes us to lash out at the world around us. Rather than judging the world outside us, we can see with the vigilant eyes of a warrior of the heart and turn our gaze inward. If we can attain a meditative state of calm and inner peace, it becomes easier to acknowledge, with radical honesty, why our emotions were roused. Shining the light on the darkness within ourselves helps us to see with greater clarity and compassion. It is an important step in taking back our own power, which includes the terrain of the many positive attributes we may have mistakenly disowned.

EXERCISING CAUTION WITH INTERACTIONS IN THE SPIRIT WORLD

We must proceed with caution when we first discover the subtle world of energy. Often, when people are craving a connection with the spiritual world or are too eager to have extrasensorial experiences, they can be led astray. Until we become versed enough in the subtle realms, it can be tricky to discern what is what.

I remember one of my students told me that he had acquired double spiritual powers since a group of disembodied souls had offered him their support. Curious, I asked why they would offer such help and soon realized that it was in exchange for animal sacrifices. Tactfully, I helped him reach the conclusion that he did not want to kill animals and that he did not want to work with spirits who would make him go against his own values.

Shamans know that we must be cautious when interacting with the invisible world. Dealing with those energies is not so different from the engagements that we find in the material world. Just as there are negative and destructive forces and people in the visible realm, there are heavy energies and hostile souls in the spiritual dimensions. For example, if we make contact with a deceased relative who was not a very kind person when they were alive and whose behavior continued to be unconscious until the end of their life, we should not be naive. We tend to operate under the assumption that the mere act of dying immediately transforms a person into a holy, conscious being. However, if the relative was abusive and greedy in this lifetime, they're likely to be the same on the other side. Instead of asking you for money, they might ask for part of your life force, which they may believe will help them out of the purgatorial realm in which they are trapped.

In shamanic terms, everything is interconnected, and our own healing has the power to ripple back to our unhealed ancestors.

While the Munay-Ki path is about being in service to the healing of all beings, healing is not about capitulating to the greedy requests of roving spirits. It is about freeing ourselves from karmic connections and toxic cords that keep us from honoring our creative life force, which can make a positive difference in this world.

I once had a client who'd been a chain-smoker since age 14, and she'd attempted to stop smoking without any success. Although her smoking was not the reason she'd come to see me, I was helping her to find balance and greater health. At some point, during a session, I could feel the presence of her deceased grandmother in the room, so I helped my client to engage in a dialogue with this spirit. We both recognized that there were old karmic connections—spiritual baggage that the grandmother had passed on to her descendants—that needed to be severed. Two weeks later, my client reached out to me to say, "Although I've always tried to quit smoking to no avail, I finally did it without even trying! I just don't have a craving for cigarettes anymore!"

My client hailed from a family that had been in the business of distributing cigarettes and alcohol in Europe for nine generations, and her grandmother had been a chain-smoker. When the karmic bond between them was removed, so was the toxic habit of smoking.

When we set boundaries with the spirit realm and affirm that our life energy is our own, we have the capacity to heal ourselves, which initiates healing backward in our ancestral lines and forward to our children's children. This is also how we establish ayni, sacred reciprocity with our ancestors—not by granting the wishes that were connected to their attachments on the earthly plane, but by addressing the wounding that continues to impact both them and us. Altars can also be a wonderful place for honoring our ancestors as well as establishing energetic boundaries around our physical and psychic space. There is an ancient Thai tradition of "spirit houses," which are shrines created to honor our ancestors and to simultaneously contain their energy so that they are not wreaking havoc in our space.

Shamanic engagement with the subtle world as well as the precautions that medicine people are trained to take in their dealings with the beings and energies that populate this realm is a subject fit for its own book (or series of books). Many people who frequently deal with the subtle realms receive rigorous training on maintaining strong boundaries as they navigate the variety of beings and intentions they might encounter. This is why it's important not to overly romanticize our engagement with the invisible realms. They are not on some faraway plane but are also right here, as part of our natural world.

It is not uncommon to find poorly trained psychics who channel wounded or needy spirits giving feeble advice. When listening to the radio, we are capable of discerning which channel has too many commercials or political views we don't agree with; thus, we keep searching until we hear just the right music or a topic of our interest. In this same way, we should learn how to tune in to the spiritual vibration that is healthiest for us.

The Seer Rite helps us discriminate between positive energies and heavy energies that are best not to engage with. In being able to discern, we simultaneously protect ourselves and avoid being overly paranoid and superstitious so that we don't assume that evil spirits are stalking us in every move.

The power of the Munay-Ki as a cohesive set of transmissions rather than a series of discontinuous rites can help us to navigate the unseen realms with the right amount of caution and respect. For example, my Bands of Power enable me to keep unwanted energies at bay, while my archetypes of the Harmony Rite refine my instinct, and the Healer Rite helps me to remember that I am working in the context of a long and protective lineage. As we continue to work with each of the Munay-Ki Rites, we naturally surround ourselves with protection as well as an enhanced sense of trust in our connection to the Great Spirit.

TRUSTING YOUR INTUITION

The Seer Rite helps us hone our connection to our intuition—the inner sight and clarity that comes from discernment. It is crucial to note that *the voice of intuition is not the same as the voice of fear.* Fear is a necessary component of our evolution as human beings, and it is useful because it can keep us out of dangerous situations. However, trauma and the lack of meaningful ways to discharge the energy that gets locked in the body after a traumatic experience can keep us in a disempowering loop of perceiving the world through fearful eyes. The Seer Rite can help us to differentiate between fear responses and the voice of our intuition, which is clear and certain, and it also allows us to move forward in our lives in ways that expand rather than shrink the heart—and that grows our faith in our own ability to make the best decisions we possibly can for ourselves.

My colleague Jill discovered how powerfully this rite could enhance her intuition:

> The balance and coherence of the *Kawak Karpay* help me work harmoniously with my heart and mind, uniting my *yachay* (right vision) with my *munay* (right action). The flavor of my life is completely different than it was before this rite. My days are drenched with meaning; I'm in ceremony in everything I do. Even amidst great challenges and transitions, I see the beauty in everything.
>
> It was not always this way. Before receiving the *Kawak Karpay*, I didn't fully trust my intuition. Decision-making was difficult for me, as doubt and lack of confidence would creep in. I'd worked in the corporate world for almost three decades when I finally burned out, entering a dark night of the soul.
>
> All along, I'd known there was more to life than the repetitive and mundane tasks I was performing—they were never fulfilling or satisfying. Eventually, these questions awoke within me: Who am I? Why am I here? What is my soul's purpose? The dawning awareness that there was more to my life than my nine-to-five job led me to the path of yoga, then shamanism.
>
> I experienced my first shamanic training with the Four Winds Society at Joshua Tree, where I immediately resonated with the teachers: powerful medicine women who owned their strength with simultaneous

humility and might. Then, when I first received the Kawak, I could see and feel my crown and necklace light up like a Christmas tree. It felt like the blinders came off, and the veil was lifted. My clairvoyance and other "sense abilities" were activated. My visual cortex, third eye, and heart were fully ignited and connected with Spirit. This rite taught me to value the coherence not only between my analytical and emotional self but also with my belly, my action center. I learned that I was taking action by not taking action; my lack of a decision was a decision in itself.

The Kawak rite also opened up my dream time. I now have vivid dreams and astrally travel with my spirit guides to the Lower and Upper worlds. My guides show me the parts of myself that still need healing, and they share information to help my community. Pachamama will often show up as chocolate, sweet breads, or wine to make me smile and remind me not to take life and myself so seriously.

The Seer's initiation also revealed my shadow side: hidden gifts and talents that I see in others but am afraid to see as my own. Like reaching a hook into the future and bringing that wisdom back into the present, I learned to reach into my own shadow, my own fertile darkness, and bring those qualities and gifts into the light so I can use them consciously as tools for myself and others. As I continue to give and receive this rite, it becomes stronger each time. My intuition now speaks to me in subtle, tuned-in ways that I trust.

THE NECESSITY OF EXPANDING OUR VISION

There is an old Hindu parable that I think of when I consider what it means to expand our vision beyond the limiting belief systems and prejudices that most of us are conditioned into. A starving family calls, "Om Namah Shivaya," which translates to, "Lord Shiva, give us a miracle." The great god Shiva shows up and offers them a boon, a divine gift. But because they are still stuck in survival-based thinking, the greatest thing they can wish for is a cartload of bread. So now, they have bread to feed the entire family for a week.

Shiva then moves on to a blind man who calls out to him: "Om Namah Shivaya." Shiva offers him a boon as well, and he says, "I would like to see my great-grandchildren eating a feast on silver plates." In one sentence, he attains a long life, love that results in not only grandchildren but great-grandchildren, a feast, abundance, and the gift of his recovered eyesight.

This story demonstrates the ways our beliefs limit or expand what is possible for us. We do not see beyond the filters of our existing belief system, and thus, what we believe we deserve or are capable of receiving. Our vision is narrowed to our conditioned views of reality.

When we expand our vision so that we can see beyond our filters, we not only become more discerning and thoughtful but also begin to see into the future, with our attention and awareness trained on what we wish to create. Rather than continuing to create based on what the people who came before us believed was possible, we choose evolution. We learn to become more aware of our blind spots and how these hinder our capacity to create a more just, free, and beautiful world for ourselves and others.

The Munay-Ki Rites show us that the reality in which we live is a co-creation between us and many seen and unseen facets of the natural and spirit realms. The Seer Rite, in particular, helps us become aware of how our belief systems are contributing to our co-creations. It also helps us envision more clearly what we want for ourselves and the world and to put our hearts and energy centers into creating from a more concrete vision. And as we take steps to expand and act on this higher vision, we make it easier for others to break out of their perceived limitations and do the same.

The Seer Rite, like all the Munay-Ki Rites, does not ask much of initiates beyond a simple dedication to feeding each transmission through one's daily experiences and interactions with the world. It was the children's book author Antoine de Saint-Exupéry who famously said, "It is only with the heart that one can see rightly; what is essential is invisible to the eye." *The Seer Rite is all about learning to see through the eyes of the heart.*

We are spiritual beings in finite human bodies, and our willingness to recognize the intrinsic impermanence of these bodies can help us engender a vision of ourselves as not just Earth beings, but galactic beings. Our destinies encompass our current realities, but they also surpass them. When we realize how brief and precious this human existence is, it gives us perspective that can help us let go of clinging and grasping to temporary conditions—and to make the best of this life, for ourselves and others.

Practice: Connect with the Eyes of the Heart

Learning to see through soft eyes is a special attribute of the shaman. It involves a combination of both peripheral (from the corners of our eyes, including the widest span of what we can see) and foveal (having a direct laser focus) vision. Soft eyes enable us to stay more relaxed—to look around us without strain or intensity so that we can take in the most information. Scientists have demonstrated that so much of what we visually absorb gets filtered out by the brain so we end up rejecting and literally not seeing anything that doesn't fit our existing worldview. Soft eyes, however, help us to experience life as a dynamic meditation. Instead of trying so hard or imposing our judgments and beliefs on what we see, we remain easeful and conscious in making our way through life. This means we can also become more open to subtle cues from the world around us. In an interesting way, soft eyes help us relax more but also remain vigilant of and in tune with our surroundings.

Take a moment to go out somewhere in nature where you can sit or lie down comfortably. Mentally connect with the lineage of Kawak and ask them to guide you to expand your capacity to "see." Let your eyes be soft; this means they won't be closed, but they won't be wide open, either. Practice letting your vision go in and out of focus until you find a relaxed gaze that can fully take in the scenery before you—not only the objects in your field of vision but also the spaces between objects, the movement of the wind through the objects, light, shadow, and so on. At a certain point, you will be looking at not only the physical trees or plants before you but also at the "energetic" imprint of the trees, which may appear as light, flickering waves or colors. As you spend more time with a soft gaze, you will learn how to focus not so directly on various forms of matter and expand your field of vision so that you can perceive the overall energy as well as phenomena of a subtle nature.

You'll also start to notice that your "vision" doesn't live in your eyes alone. Your subtle perception may make itself known in other ways, such as a tingling sensation on your skin or an awareness in your gut. Notice how nonvisual information is relayed through your body and mind and how the practice of maintaining a soft gaze also helps you to access invisible cues from your environment.

Chapter 5:

THE
DAYKEEPER RITE

*Don't judge each day for the harvest you reap but by
the seeds that you plant.*

— ROBERT LOUIS STEVENSON

The next Munay-Ki transmission is the Daykeeper Rite, or Pampa
Mesayok Karpay. This rite invites the initiate into a vibrant lineage of master healers who embody an ever-flowing dialogue with
the spirit of Earth, Pachamama, renewing the nourishing and sustaining power of all life. The Daykeeper salutes each sunrise and
makes offerings and prayers for the day to flow in sacred order and
ayni. They bring balance to the land and community by activating the elements on their altars and by feeding and honoring the
spirits of nature.

A Daykeeper has cultivated enough love, wisdom, and strength
to transcend the little "me" and become a medicine person for the
community. This encompasses humans, animals, plants, and all
nature. The Daykeeper has developed the skill and intention to
move less from an egocentric place and more from a place that is
concerned with the interconnectedness of our daily lives—with
what is best for *all of us.* This is clear in the moment-to-moment
decisions that a Daykeeper makes, as they recognize that their
individual well-being is not separate from the well-being of their

community. At this stage, the process of healing transcends self-absorbed desires, even the desire to be a "better person." When everyone in the ecosystem experiences better health, Pachamama's resources flow more abundantly and the entire community benefits: if there are more flowers, there are more bees and more honey for everyone.

This does not mean that, as Daykeepers, we fail to attend to our own health, wants, and needs. It is absolutely imperative that we continue to care for ourselves. We must allow our cup of abundance to fill so that it can naturally overflow and benefit others; we must feel the harmony and goodness in our own lives so that we can better share it. Daykeepers recognize the ongoing process of personal growth and healing, but this coincides with the journey of bringing healing and balance to the whole—for individual well-being and collective well-being feel one and the same when we practice them authentically.

The Daykeeper enjoys a sense of purpose, but this role is not about fulfilling the need to be useful, which is too often tied to limiting cultural beliefs about the importance of productivity in order to feel a sense of worth and belonging. Instead, when we are firmly established in our own intrinsic value and no longer grasping for external validation to help us feel okay about ourselves, we can be truly present and fully contribute to helping our surroundings.

This is where genuine, rather than performative, love and care for ourselves, the land, and all of Pachamama's inhabitants come rushing in. The Daykeeper strives to maintain a sense of integrity that comes from a connection to munay—the universal principle of love—so that they can be a light in the community and an oasis of consciousness.

Reciprocity and harmony, which are core components of all the Munay-Ki Rites, now bring us into alignment with the feminine aspect of the Great Spirit—with the aspect of life that is maternal and cyclical. As Daykeepers, we feel attuned to the seasons and cycles of nature. We notice as certain flowers wilt and others blossom in the sun. We notice when the day brings the songs of the birds and the awakening of many insects and four-legged creatures. And when the sun sets, we glimpse the glowing eyes of nocturnal animals, the rhythms of moonlight, and night-blooming plants. We recognize that all these phenomena are essential to the rich tapestry of creation, and we make a commitment to preserving the delicate balance that is inherent in each complex layer of the web of life.

When offering this rite, the shaman touches the right and left sides of the body (solar/masculine and lunar/feminine) to create balance; and then taps on the initiate's head, heart, and belly to bring coherence between the three centers. This is followed by the actual transmission of the lineage—forehead to forehead.

ORIGINS OF THE DAYKEEPER RITE: ENSURING AYNI WITH THE LAND

Pampa Mesayok comes from three linguistic roots. In Spanish, the word *pampa* refers to an extensive grass-covered plain; the Andean peoples used the term to refer to any flat area that is good for grazing animals or growing crops. The word evokes a womb-like place of fertile earth that grows food for the community. *Mesa* refers to the shaman's altar, the collection of stones that anchor the shaman's wisdom and connection to ancestors, the natural realm, and dimensions beyond ordinary reality. The stones on the mesa are also connected to the sacred mountains from which the shamans source insight and power and to the natural elements (such as lightning or water) that shaped the stones. Finally, *yok* means "power," and the quality of this power is connected to how the shamans embody the medicine they have secured in their altars.

The Pampa Mesayok has an intimate connection with the bounty of Pachamama and maintains an altar for the well-being of the community. Far beyond helping a single neighbor or the friend of a friend, the Pampa Mesayok serves the area, the *pampa*, or in Quechua, the *ayllu*—the entire community. In this way, each community needs their own Pampa Mesayok who sustains and nurtures ayni with the land. They also greet the light of the day and act as a keeper of the seasons. For this reason, the English translation of this rite is "Daykeeper."

The Pampa Mesayok is responsible for maintaining ayni with the land—for making offerings to Pachamama and asking for her blessings and nourishment. Just as the Seer Rite awakens clear inner and outer vision, the Daykeeper Rite awakens the power of profound listening. This is not the kind of listening that comes from our ears alone, but from all our senses. The Pampa Mesayok learn to attend to the subtle whisperings of nature, which gives them the knowledge they need to cultivate a healthy balance for their village and to reestablish well-being when it is lost. They are familiar with nature's various cycles, including peak expression at midday or during the summer as well as moments for pause and restoration, like in the darkness of the night and the depths of winter.

The Pampa Mesayok recognizes that everything that sustains the human body comes from the Earth Mother: food, clothing, shelter, and means of travel—and the inspiration from all her magnificent expressions of beauty in nature. Further, they know that they are one with the elements (earth, fire, water, air, and pure light), and they live this through every encounter with the land. For them, each step on this Earth is sacred. In pilgrimages and dances, they caress the land with their feet, and as they walk, they sustain an ever-flowing conversation with nature.

In early times, the Pampa Mesayok attended to stone altars, like the ones found in Machu Picchu and all over the Inka Empire. Highly attuned to the cyclical nature of life, they celebrated ceremonies to prepare the land and sow the seeds for a healthy harvest. When they needed something, they gave Pachamama an offering; they did not simply look for or take things without acknowledging her sovereignty. The Pampa Mesayok listened to nature—to the herbs, flowers, crops, and animals—and respected the age-old wisdom of how to grow food, how to coax life out of the soil, and how to give life back to Pachamama. This reciprocal cycle of giving and receiving was central to the Pampa Mesayok's livelihood and service to their community.

Still today, the Pampa Mesayok makes offerings to ensure an auspicious planting, harvesting, or gathering. When people build new stone huts, ceremonies ensure there is respect for the site itself, and honor is given to the land on which the building stands; such ceremonies bring peace to the spirits of the place in the invisible world. Because the Andean peoples are herders, the Pampa Mesayok also makes offerings for the safety and well-being of the animals. This offering is often known as *despacho* in Spanish or *haywarikuy* in Quechua.

There are wonderful gifts that emerge from such deep listening. The Andean medicine men and women still feel the pulse of life in all nature and are known for their ability to speak with plant spirits. Most often, they carry a bundle of coca leaves that they chew for stamina while they walk in high altitudes, and they anchor their prayers in the leaves and put them in their mouths to commune with the great spirits of the heavens, the mountains, and the land.

SOUL RETRIEVAL AND CEREMONY

The Pampa Mesayok's abilities are further developed than those of the healer. For example, in the Andes, they perform soul retrieval, which is necessary when parts of a person's soul have become lost or fragmented because of pain or trauma. In this ritual, the Pampa Mesayok gives a *haywaricuy*, an offering to Pachamama, asking her to aid in the returning of the lost soul.

The Pampa Mesayok's connection to the natural world also offers them the gift of prophecy. On one occasion, I ran into a shaman who, just hours before, had been in a bus accident where a few people were seriously hurt. Luckily, he was uninjured, yet, when we met, his heart was beating louder than usual and his eyes were wide open (as if still looking at the accident). In broken Spanish, he recounted the event for me, and at the end he said, "I knew something bad would happen. The coca was bitter that morning."

Pampa Mesayok routinely use coca leaves as an oracle by praying to the spirit of the plant as well as to heavenly and earthly spirits before wrapping the leaves in a ceremonial cloth. By tasting the coca and interpreting the patterns of the leaves on the cloth, they can track the past and foretell the future.

The universal Daykeeper also prays for goodness to enter the homes and hearts of the community: not just people, but nature, animals, and all beings, from the visible and invisible worlds. Beyond an intellectual idea of "we are all one," the Daykeeper carries a deep understanding that the children of the community are also their children. The grandparents are also their grandparents. The ancestors, collectively speaking, are their ancestors. There is an awareness that we must all move toward wellness together.

THE ONE WHO SPEAKS WITH THE LAND

Many of us in the Western world live in cities or suburbs surrounded by cement. As we cultivate a connection with the Daykeeper Rite, we begin to notice the rising and setting of the sun and the phases of the moon. We become more attuned to our circadian rhythms and natural cycles by sleeping when it's best for our body and waking up to birdsong and the first light of the day. We might wish to fill our home with more living things by bringing in flowers or plants. We also increase our awareness of how the environment influences our mood, our thoughts, and the evolution of our emotions throughout the day. As we attune to life's rhythms, we also grow curious about our food: Where does it come from? What nutrients does it contain? We will notice when our food feels vibrant—because it comes from healthy crops, attended to with love—or when it feels devoid of energy and life.

This awareness is key to the Daykeeper initiation. As we come into a more awakened relationship with Pachamama, we begin embodying more health and consciousness, which enables us to be a light for others. There is a coherence between what we think, say, feel, and do. For example, the veganism movement gained traction in the last 20 years, with activists and experts in the fields of health sharing information about how we can address the topic of animal consumption and the toll it has taken on our world.

This movement has revealed uncomfortable truths about the meat industry and revelatory ones about how plant-based diets can transform our individual and societal health. As Daykeepers, we may choose to enlighten others, but this must begin with embodying what we believe—and not just preaching. As we radiate more health, contentment, and truth, people notice and become curious, drawn as if by a magnetic force.

We also realize that no matter what we do to pay our bills at the end of the month, it is important that our overall contribution be positive for our community and the environment. We feel the need to give back to the Earth to show our love. For example, if I work in a hospital and notice that there are instances of malpractice, I might speak up or refuse to act in unethical ways. If I work in law, I might turn down a client whose actions infringe on the rights of a minority, or I might be courageous enough to blow the whistle on a corporation that poisons the water or air.

It is important to recognize that the Daykeeper does not pay lip service to the idea of "oneness" or choose to stay in a comfort zone and ignore injustice or engage in spiritual bypassing. Rather, we become more discerning of the ripples that our actions create. The Daykeeper is not merely a nice ideal or intellectual construct, nor is it overindulgent or false positivity. It is a transmission that brings us into greater integrity with ourselves and our planet; it instigates us to embody our values rather than simply saying the right words.

CONNECTING TO THE GREAT MOTHER

The Daykeeper Rite encourages engagement with the sacred feminine, or the Great Mother archetype, which is necessary today for the healing and transformation of the world and our planetary consciousness. It is important to remember that the Great Mother is a part of you, as you are a part of her. As the primordial mother of all creation, she is the one from whom all our gifts arise, and she asks that we share these gifts with the world. She invites us to discover that everything we need for our healing is available to us, in forms ranging from plant medicine to the innovations that stem from our ever-evolving understanding of our extraordinary planet.

Alberto understood that in order to become a Daykeeper, we must attend to our unresolved issues with our mothers and the feminine as well as the hurts within us that long for the healing touch of the Universal Mother:

> We were with a group of my students and friends, accompanied by four master shamans who had walked with us from the mountain Ausangate to the old hacienda belonging to my friend Américo Yabar and his family. The hacienda included the land of the Q'ero nation and by now was a cluster of decrepit and collapsing old adobe structures. Outside, the grass had been kept neatly trimmed by a half dozen alpacas, and the maqui trees were laden with fruit. The Mappocho River raged wildly a thousand feet below.
>
> That afternoon, we were to receive the Pampa Mesayok rites as the sun began to dip low in the horizon, and Américo would be helping translate the significance of the initiation. Don Mariano Apaza, the eldest of the paq'os [Andean shaman] explained that this was the rite to awaken the sacred dialogue with the mother. That sounded great to me, but I did not like what I heard next.
>
> "It brings up your unresolved issues with the feminine," the old man said.
>
> I was hoping that at this point I would germinate these seeds painlessly and miraculously, without any effort on my part. No free ride, I reminded myself.
>
> I reflected on how we usually keep our own hurt places and wounds hidden, often even from ourselves. With time, I would understand that the Pampa Mesayok rites made non-ordinary resources available to you. These included the power of nature and the wisdom of the Mother. These would assist you in your healing journey and help you to become whole.

A profound honoring of the Great Mother is necessary for those who wish to become stewards of her life-giving energy. From the moment we met, one of my students, Sebastian, displayed a keen sensibility and understanding of the feminine principle. His dedication to the Great Mother made it clear that he was a Daykeeper at heart, and he quickly came to understand the

Munay-Ki Rites in depth and became one of our most respected teachers. In his words:

> Before I encountered this rite, I was initiated into a spiritual path that centered on the image of the Goddess as the creator of all life. In 2013, I began searching for land on which to build a temple in honor of the Goddess. I yearned to create both a devotional space and a mystery school, but after an intense, several-year search, I could not find the right place.
>
> In 2015, I received the Munay-Ki Rites at the Los Lobos Sanctuary, in Chile, where the Pampa Mesayok transmission touched me most powerfully. Its connection to Pachamama and the lineages of women and men who guard the stone altars resonated with my previous connection with the Great Mother, making this experience profound and sacred. After receiving the rites, I made a despacho, and my main focus of prayers was directed to the Pampa Mesayok lineage. Only a few weeks after returning from Chile and making this offering, my ardent search concluded—I found the beautiful place where my Temple of the Goddess is now located.
>
> With the temple came a renewed commitment to life to my spiritual path and to the responsibility of caring for the land where it is located: a rainforest whose acreage has been diminishing due to livestock activity. The small patches of primary rainforest around and even inside the temple represent true sanctuaries for species that are increasingly disturbed by human activities. This initiation has prompted me to constantly educate myself and provide to that ecosystem what it needs; it has also helped me encourage city visitors away from heavy consumerist habits and toward actions that are more friendly with the environment.
>
> The Pampa Mesayok rite inspired me to establish more stable relationships with the spirits and allies within the landscape. The temple has offered a space where I can appreciate nature in a less romanticized and more concrete dimension, contemplating with curiosity the peculiarities of an ecosystem and learning about its way of being. It has been and continues to be a constant learning where the weather, the winds, and the fleeting appearance of certain wild animals are great teachers.
>
> From the regular practice of offerings, the care of the altar, and the guidance I receive from the Pampa Mesayok lineage, I always gain useful insights.

GIVING BACK TO THE COMMUNITY AND THE LAND

The Daykeeper lineage helps us to become more aware of the vast and mysterious terrain of Mother Earth and all her living beings. We see life as a continuum between the seen and unseen realms, which helps us become more discerning of our impact to the intricate web of existence. We discover ourselves within this web, and we behold our own unique gifts and qualities that allow us to contribute meaningfully and "light up" the part of the web that contains us.

Modern society often encourages volunteerism as a way of "giving back" to a cause or community. However, some people might volunteer in a transactional way—to prove they're a "good person" or "generous" or because they want others to see them as an ally or leader. This is a start, but when our hearts see from the eyes of a Daykeeper, we show up with sincerity and enthusiasm according to our possibilities. As an example, let's say I find my gift is physical strength—this might lead me to become a firefighter. Or perhaps my calling comes when I am older and less physically agile: I might read books or tell stories to the children at my local library once a week. If activism and standing for a cause feels right for me, I might plant trees and create more green spaces in my urban community. All these nurturing actions come from the awareness that the health of my community is my health.

When I was younger, I never thought about cultivating an intimate relationship with the land. I never dreamed that one day I would grow my own vegetables or tend to many trees or chickens, dogs, and other animals. This was not something that I aspired to in my youth when I pursued adventure sports. I used to enjoy nature as a means to an end—to fulfill my own needs for food, inspiration, pleasure, and comfort. I relished the sunrise and sunset while I surfed Pacific Ocean waves, and while those sports felt good and healthy, I never thought of offering incense, a prayer, or a despacho back to nature to express my gratitude. I simply took. The world was my oyster, for me to enjoy, but it never occurred to me that I could give back.

By the time Alberto and I moved to Chile, I had new priorities in life, and together we built a sanctuary to cultivate and share wisdom—a place where we would welcome teachers and students. As we planned the building of the facilities (housing and a teaching hall), I had to pay attention to the trajectory of the sun for the sake of how to orient the structures and where to place the windows. And as we landscaped with the help of an ecologist, I began learning about soil and ecosystems. Within this atmosphere, and while admiring the bumblebees and hummingbirds, the Daykeeper's seeds began blossoming with full force, and I longed to immerse my hands in the earth. Soon, I was planting flowers and, in a joint effort with our neighbors, I cultivated a large vegetable garden. Gradually we also planted over a thousand trees to help re-forest the area. Throughout the different seasons of the year, we harvest a great variety of herbs, vegetables, and fruits.

I feel really grateful about these experiences, knowing that it is not always easy to go with nature's flow and to experience the power of community. In much of the modern world, we are disconnected from the sources of our food; instead of knowing the farmers who grow and pick the fruits and vegetables we eat, we buy from supermarkets where produce sits for days under fluorescent lights. Furthermore, many people eliminate fresh fruits and vegetables from their diet—opting for easy microwaveable TV dinners, processed food, and fast food. We live in a culture of convenience that has zapped much of the vitality from what we take in as nourishment, so it is little wonder that dis-ease and illness abound in the so-called developed world.

Since my diet is mostly vegan and gluten-free, I rarely go out to restaurants while at home in Chile because most places focus on meat or pasta. However, if I choose to eat out, I patronize the restaurant of a woman named Rosita, who clearly embodies the spirit of the Daykeeper. Rosita truly cares about nourishing her clientele, not just stuffing people's bellies. She is open only on weekends because during the rest of the week, she is personally selecting the local produce that she will prepare in her kitchen. Rosita doesn't have a set menu but finds creative ways to prepare the treasures that she finds at farmers' markets and organic super-markets. She is also very conscious when it comes to celebrating days that are special to her customers. I remember inviting my father to lunch on Father's Day, and as we enjoyed our delicious meal, Rosita stepped out of the kitchen and offered a heartfelt speech honoring all fathers before welcoming a band that played live music to commemorate the day.

It is not a fancy place, but it is teeming with personality, from the antique bikes and artifacts hanging from a tall ceiling to the paintings by local artists that fill the walls. The small but beautiful gardens are full of hummingbirds and bees buzzing, and there is a lively pond of white and pink water lilies. Rosita doesn't advertise her eatery, and it doesn't even have a sign with a name on it. All her customers have learned about her through word of mouth, and they gather to experience her loving heart, which is obvious in her demeanor and in her food. She has created community in a small rural town where ancestral rituals have been forgotten and there is a great need for Daykeepers. Rosita doesn't merely cook; she presides over a sacred space where everyone who enters feels nourished.

You don't have to move to the country and grow potatoes or corn or open your own restaurant to live in reciprocity with the land and your community; you can simply start by cultivating an intentional relationship with nature, wherever you are. Be conscious of the sunrise and begin making contact with our magnificent sun. And when the clouds arrive, be grateful for the water in the skies, for the fire energy of lightning, and for the way these elements live in your body.

No matter where you are in the world, you can open your heart to say thank you for all the blessings of the day. You can cultivate a sense of humus (the organic, loamy soil from which all things grow), remembering that you are a body teeming with all the elements as well as an infinite being. You are life itself. This understanding alone has profound implications for the ways we might enter a more reciprocal relationship with nature and others.

Practice: Become a Sacred Witness

The Daykeeper recognizes that the very facet of human life is a miracle in and of itself, and you can practice becoming a sacred witness to the miraculous. Greet the rising sun each morning—for it's truly a miracle that we exist in this solar system in a balance of perfect conditions that enable our planet to rotate at just the right distance from the sun for life as it is to be possible. As you greet and thank the sun, set an intention to be the best human being you can be for the day ahead: to make the best use of your time, to serve your community in the highest ways possible, to face your challenges with courage and equanimity, and to offer kindness and encouragement to your neighbors.

To affirm this intention, light a candle to bring the light of the sun to your own space, awakening the warm and healing light within your own being. In Mexican pre-Columbian art, you find beautiful candleholders of multiple figures holding hands and embracing one another in a circle. This represents the community, and the light that is placed at its center represents the light of the Daykeeper, who is committed not only to their own individual journey but also to cultivating the joy and vitality of the land and all beings.

Chapter 6:

THE WISDOMKEEPER RITE

The more we know, the more we love.
The more we love, the more we know.

— RAMAKRISHNA

The Wisdomkeeper Rite, or Alto Mesayok Karpay, grows from the day-to-day sustenance the Daykeeper Rite provides. The seeds of the Wisdomkeeper begin to germinate as the initiate ascends the metaphorical mountain that connects the lands with the heavens. For the people of the Andes, mountains contain fathomless wisdom; they took millions of years to evolve into the majestic peaks they are today. Thus, the Wisdomkeeper communes with the essence of the planet. They can feel the power of the minerals, the bones of the earth, and the spirit that resides within and towers above Pachamama.

The Wisdomkeeper understands that the mountain is their altar, and it connects the primordial essence of nature with the cosmic mystery of the Great Spirit. The Wisdomkeeper knows their mountain, for they have traveled there on pilgrimages and made offerings; when they pray, they do so as if they were standing at the summit, or nestled inside a mountain cave, even if their body is physically elsewhere. The vision, love, and power of the Wisdomkeeper are sustained by the apu—the tutelary spirit of the mountain who serves as a protector or guardian.

In the Introduction of this book, I shared my first pilgrimage to a mountain; this was an excursion of prayer and communion with the elements of nature. Prior to this experience, I tended to visit mountains with the intention of hiking, skiing, or conquering difficult terrain. But during my pilgrimage, I learned about surrender and what it means to listen to the wild, undomesticated voice of the apus. Just as the Daykeeper initiation connects us to the nurturing wisdom of the feminine principle, the Wisdomkeeper initiation connects us to the protective and visionary primordial masculine. In time, we develop inner strength, confidence, and leadership skills, and we feel confident to sustain our path, especially when "the going gets tough." The mountain's sturdiness offers a sense of grounding so that the initiate can feel safe and protected by summoning the apu and visualizing the body of the mountain surrounding them.

The Wisdomkeeper's horizon extends to a broader swath of time and space. This doesn't mean that they see everything that happens within that swath, but their awareness of what matters informs their words and deeds as well as the way they move in the world. A Wisdomkeeper's higher vision can see through the difficulties and challenges of ordinary reality, beyond the "flat lands" and into other terrains. Regardless of tradition or religious orientation, Wisdomkeepers recognize one another, a silent recognition that flashes between them as they see themselves working in tandem to keep sacred and alive the most delicate of spiritual truths.

This rite is offered in the same way as the Daykeeper Rite; that is, the shaman touches the right and left sides of the body (solar/masculine and lunar/feminine) and taps on the initiate's head, heart, and belly. This is followed by the actual transmission of the lineage—forehead to forehead. Though the rite can be transmitted from mentor to mentee, it is also possible that the medicine person organically communes with the apus of the mountain, and the initiate is offered the rite directly by Spirit.

In the Munay-Ki, we transmit this rite as if giving a beautiful ceremonial garment to someone that they will have to grow into; we give them the seed, then tell them how to nurture this seed so that it will blossom. This rite is transmitted with the hope that the recipient will reach their full spiritual potential as a Wisdomkeeper someday.

ORIGINS OF THE WISDOMKEEPER RITE: A HEART AS STRONG AS A MOUNTAIN

The Wisdomkeeper is known as the Alto Mesayok in the Andes. *Alto* is the Spanish word for "high," evoking the majestic stature of the apus. *Mesa* is the altar on which Andean shamans keep their medicine stones and amulets. *Yok* is "power" in the Quechua language. Thus, the Alto Mesayok is the person who receives wisdom and power from the high mountains and from the apus.

In the Andean tradition, a sign that a person has been offered the Wisdomkeeper Rite is when they are struck by lightning and survive. Lore says this person has been rewired by the apus and the heavens. If the person is new to the medicine path, they are destined to become an Alto Mesayok; they will be urged (by life, circumstances, the spirit world, intuition, community, lineage, and so on) to take the journey home to this lineage. It may require years of learning, but eventually, they will discover how to listen and speak to the apus and perhaps develop the power and wisdom to summon lightning at will and to change the weather.

In the Andean world today, when a person is struck by lightning, they rarely survive. The mountain people have adopted modern customs, including the clothes they wear and the items they carry. Their shoes contain metal nails (in contrast to the rubber sandals of their ancestors), and they are likely to have keys, pocketknives, and cellphones on them, all of which conduct electricity. Unfortunately, the lives of men and women who may have been destined for a shamanic path are cut short.

Andean lore also speaks of accomplished Alto Mesayoks who survived not just one but several lightning strikes and embodied the power to bring Heaven to Earth—that is, to manifest in the flesh what is dreamed in the world of spirit.

When speaking of Alto Mesayoks within the Munay-Ki, we are referring to what is considered the highest level in the Andean tradition: the "Suyu" Alto Mesayok. Those whose power reaches a vast region beyond the immediate community *(ayllu)* and beyond various lands and villages *(llakta)*. In this sense, the Alto Mesayok is directly guided by the apu to be attentive to not only the short term but also a longer time, not merely for immediate benefit but for the benefit of children in the future.

The Alto Mesayok usually has one primary apu, but they can source from many mountains, just like we may have many elderly relatives but have one who acts specifically as a godmother or god-father, a guardian to whom we are closest. My second time on a pilgrimage to connect with an apu was to Ausangate, a sacred mountain for the local people, and Alberto's apu and the "god-father" of the Munay-Ki. Alberto made multiple pilgrimages to this mountain to receive many of the transmissions that would become a part of the Munay-Ki Rites. When his mentor, Don Manuel, decided it was time to ask for a new rite to prepare people for the challenging times ahead, they went to Ausangate to offer their prayers.

Many years ago, I had the experience, in dreamtime, of seeing the face of this mountain, which is said to be very auspicious. Alberto had prayed to Ausangate to transmit to me the wisdom and strength to continue the path he'd laid for Western shamanic practitioners. This was when Ausangate showed me his wise and compassionate grandfather face—the light and the shadows in its glacier revealed his eyes, nose, mouth, and wrinkles, framed by his snow-white hair and beard. Then, without words, but with a feeling, he said, "I will protect you!"

Even now, in times when I feel vulnerable, I call upon Apu Ausangate and feel his embrace, as if my body itself becomes the mountain, and I am held in its wisdom, love, and robustness.

On one occasion when I felt my entire world collapsing, the only thing left standing was Apu Ausangate.

MOUNTAIN OFFERINGS

Throughout history there are plenty of stories of mountains as sacred pilgrimage sites—a place for vision quests in which the veils between the worlds become thinner and one can feel closer to Spirit. Let's remember Moses receiving the Ten Commandments at Mount Sinai as part of the covenant between God and the Israelites: "Moses spoke, and God answered him in thunder. The Lord came down on Mount Sinai, to the top of the mountain. And the Lord called Moses to the top of the mountain, and Moses went up" (Exodus 19: 16–20).

We can also think of the sacred Mount Kailash, which Hindus revere as the abode of the god Shiva and as the earthly manifestation of the mythic Mount Meru—the spiritual center of the universe for the Bön and the Tibetan Buddhists. Thousands of devotees each year complete the 32-mile ritual circumambulation of this mountain, taking anywhere from one day of fast walking to a whole month of full-body prostrations. Either way, incense, bells, ritual chants, and tsampa are constant offerings.

In Hawaii, the volcanoes are the embodiment of the goddess Pelehonuamea, "she who shapes the sacred land," by sending rivers of lava down the mountain sides. She is revered by the natives of the islands as both creatrix and the destroyer, and she is offered fruit, flowers, berries, and other forest plants.

Unfortunately, in our modern times, connection to the mountains has been for the most part forgotten or compromised, except when Indigenous spirituality has remained alive. Returning to the Andes, we can reflect on how, long ago, it used to take at least a week to travel from the city of Cusco to the Q'ero mountainous villages on foot. When the Spanish conquistadors brought horses and mules, travel time was reduced. When the roads were paved, you could still only get so far; after a certain point, you had to walk to or from the mountain for two days. When the mining companies came, eager to extract minerals, they paved all the way to the main Q'ero village. Recently, when I asked Don Pascual Apaza how the digging was going, he shared with a laugh that one of the apus, called Huamanlipa, had not given the miners permission. Thus, the mining companies found nothing (no gold, no minerals), and they ceased all digging. Don Pascual believed that the apu was protecting their village and his people. This story demonstrates that even with the ravages of mining and human greed, the medicine people from these mountains have maintained a relationship with the apu, who has been protecting their village, from the Spanish conquistadors to modern-day corporations.

The Alto Mesayok forges a relationship with the apu by asking what the mountain would like from the people, and the apu can request specific offerings. The Alto Mesayok then makes these offerings in a ceremony rich with humbleness and gratitude. Oftentimes, over a traditional cloth or a modern gift paper, with great delicacy they arrange all kinds of little items that symbolize their prayers—from grains and flowers to say thank you to miniature animals or houses to ask for abundance. In this way, the Altomesayok honors and speaks to their mountain and, being truly connected, also hear the apu answering with inspiration and guidance.

When Alberto developed a relationship with the apu of Ausangate four decades ago, he began receiving instruction on the Munay-Ki Rites (before they were given a name). He returned to Ausangate almost every year since then—and it is through the medicine and insights he receives from Ausangate that he has guided the Munay-Ki.

WHEN METAPHORICAL LIGHTNING STRIKES

The Wisdomkeeper initiation looks different for those of us who do not live in villages in the high mountains. It is rarely a literal lightning strike; instead, the transmission comes from more metaphorical lightning, and it means that we have a disposition for this.

When we say yes to this rite, we are ready to awaken our hearts to be of service, to become part of a lineage that guides us toward wisdom, and to devote ourselves to growing into the larger garments of the Wisdomkeeper and beyond.

The proverbial lightning strike for most of us in the modern world could come in the form of a crisis that sends us to the ER, or the death of a loved one, or a divorce that leaves us shattered. Like being struck by lightning, we can either view these crisis moments as life-breaking or path-making. We can lose our sense of hope and trust in life, failing to recognize the initiation at hand that is inviting us into a new way of being, or we can survive the lightning strike and take it as an opportunity to rebuild anew—to discover our innate strength and courage as well as our ability to make more life-affirming choices.

I recently read about an influencer from Mexico who was stabbed and abused by her attacker. Yet, instead of succumbing to fear and the stark reality of living in a violent society, she became a guide for many others. Her spirit could not be crushed. She declared to the world: "No, this cannot be the end of the road for me. Life is beautiful, and I intend to see and cherish its beauty." Despite the suffering she'd been through, she became a vessel for joy and hope—an example of what it means to continually choose life-affirming values instead of becoming weighed down by the agonies that may visit us along our human path. She not only survived the lightning strike but also allowed herself to be rewired by it. And in this way, she became a guide for others who may have experienced similar despair.

Crises can offer great opportunities for wisdom that we may not have previously had access to, such as a newfound compassion or a mindset through which we can grow into a more transpersonal life and a deeper connection with the Great Spirit.

In dealing with the metaphorical lightning strikes, we can recognize that the fire that nearly destroyed us in the process also has the capacity to give us new life. When we transmute painful life lessons by finding their hidden gifts, we harness the energy of the lightning and reclaim our power to make positive things happen. Many Wisdomkeepers are able to find a way forward from traumatic experiences and guide and inspire others by sharing their stories of resilience and reinvention. This kind of sharing empowers others toward selfless, courageous action that can serve to build a healthier society.

You may wish to consider some of the challenging experiences that have touched your own life. Do you continue to stew in resentment and self-pity? Or, with the strength of a mountain, have you transformed your personal lightning strikes into opportunities to empower yourself and others?

However, not all metaphorical lightning strikes occur in the form of a painful crisis. They can also be strikes of luck, great realizations of truths, epiphanies, even divine blessings. As an example, we can think of Paul the Apostle's transformation after the legendary "road to Damascus" event—when Paul, previously known as Saul, was on his way to arrest followers of Jesus to return with them to Jerusalem for punishment, and he was suddenly dazzled by a light. According to the Acts of the Apostles (9:4–5) in the New Testament: "He fell to the ground and heard a voice say to him, 'Saul, Saul, why do you persecute me?'

'Who are you, Lord?' Saul asked.

'I am Jesus, whom you are persecuting,' he replied."

For three days, Saul was blind, and he did not eat or drink until he was cured in Damascus by a disciple of Christ. After these events, Saul was baptized, beginning immediately to spread Jesus's teachings to the Gentiles (the non-Jews) and became known as Saint Paul.

REINTEGRATING THE DIVINE MASCULINE

Just as Alberto and Sebastian discovered a deeper connection to the Great Mother through the Daykeeper Rite, many initiates to the Wisdomkeeper Rite discover a new blessed relationship with the archetypal Father and with their inner masculine. This clearly happened to Antonella, one of my students who came to our school in Chile about six years ago and today teaches with us. She rediscovered her own wholeness in the wake of the Wisdomkeeper initiation. She says:

> The Alto Mesayok brought awareness to an ache I did not realize I had. As a child, I was very close with my father; our bond was special and precious to me. When I was seven years old, he suffered an aneurysm, and in an instant, I lost my father. He didn't die, but the aneurysm changed him entirely. When he came back from surgery, he was a stranger to me: bald, with a large scar across his entire head, unable to speak well. Who is this? I thought. Our connection was severed completely.
>
> After his aneurysm, my mother had to step up for me and my brothers to provide for and support us. She wrestled with a lot of fear, so I grew up without that masculine stability and encouragement to go forth and take risks. I had no sense of a sturdy rock beneath me from which I could fly into my life.
>
> When I was 18, my father died, and my wounds were invisible to me for many years. Unconsciously, I sought ways of bringing masculine energy into my life to support me as I accomplished things; from romantic partners to friendships, I have searched for that strong energy to ground me. For many years, I felt lonely and somewhat disconnected—with an emptiness inside me, a missing piece within me, a deep sorrow.
>
> When I encountered the Alto Mesayok, it opened the door for me to heal my relationship with masculine energy, especially my wounded part that felt fatherless. Now, I move through life feeling the firmness of the mountains on my back and the knowledge that they accompany me, no matter what. The mountains talk to each other and hold sacred space for us just by being there. I walk more confidently, knowing that I am not alone.
>
> This rite also invites me to become comfortable with discomfort. I am not a sporty person; in my life, I try not to be uncomfortable . . . On a pilgrimage to the high mountains, every step challenged me. I proceeded with masculine energy, knowing that physical discomfort was part of the journey: a sacrifice, not in a negative way, but as in [the original meaning of] "making sacred." Every step taught me that it's okay to be uncomfortable. The discomfort can be an offering in itself.
>
> Like all the rites of the Munay-Ki, this experience took me to an inner place of responsibility . . . I not only spend my time healing myself, but I also open my eyes, own my role as a steward of the earth, and take action. I remember to ask myself if there's something within me or in my reach that needs to come back to balance so I can act on it, maybe by

having a conversation, setting boundaries, or letting go—none of which are easy to do. But when I ask for assistance from the forces around me, and the lineages, I can trust and let myself be guided.

Now, I feel whole every time I'm in ceremony, connecting with the mountains with a despacho or by calling them when I blow a kintu. Now, every time I pray to the mountains of the place where I was born, I feel at home again. I feel that the seed of the Alto Mesayok opened my heart to receive all the love of nature that has always been there for me, waiting patiently.

In working with the Wisdomkeeper lineage and with the spirit of the mountain, we may feel a new sense of courage and strength while feeling protected and inspired. We live in a society that tends to value what are considered masculine traits over the feminine, but in truth, it also distorts the masculine to the point of equating strength and power with violence and brute force. While true strength carries authority with it, it is also about honor and a larger responsibility to one's community and the planet. The divine masculine does not seek to degrade or dominate the feminine; rather, these two integral parts of our being complement each other and contribute to our wholeness.

COMMITTING TO SERVICE AND CARE

Just like the Daykeeper, the Wisdomkeeper contemplates life beyond a purely personal, self-centered attitude. It is not only about *me*, but about *us*. This sense of caring goes beyond one's immediate, nuclear community.

At the same time, while their purview may be large, the Wisdomkeeper understands that they must narrow their focus to the themes that are important to them in order to be most effective. For example, if they are concerned about reforestation or about water rights for animals and people, the lineage will guide the Wisdomkeeper to study what may be happening in neighboring communities and around the world with respect to these topics.

These days, we are accustomed to consuming a lot of superfluous information. With the deluge of messages from social media, the news, and every passing trend that emerges and fades back into the marketplace of ideas, we compile facts (many of them meaningless or only partially true) in the same way a computer might gather data on a hard drive. This doesn't make us wise, though. In the spirit of the munay that lives within the Wisdomkeeper, knowledge is meant to serve life; it is meant to feed the children, shelter the poor, heal the sick, protect the animals, preserve nature, and contribute to the preservation of our complex and interconnected ecosystems.

The Wisdomkeepers of the Andes recognized that "the more we know and the more we love," the more we are called to attend to the most pressing needs of our times. This is an organic feeling that arises from the experience of munay. Pure love urges us to be in service when and where we can, without becoming a martyr or a victim (an identity that the Healer Rite helps us to release).

I recently felt the love and wisdom of the Wisdomkeeper lineage in a dream. For a bit of context, in the past three years, I have observed how the drug cartels from Colombia and Venezuela have made their way into Ecuador, Peru, and Chile, where I have a home. This has been particularly distressing lately, as the level of violence has risen tremendously.

In my dream, I arrived at a beautiful and secluded beach with my extended family—about 15 of us. We were delighted as we played on the shore and swam in clear, refreshing waters. Soon, a group of narcos (people involved with the cartel) with guns came and demanded all our money. Without protesting, we gave them everything we had. At this point, I believed they would let us go in peace. However, they wanted me and a couple of others to remain as hostages. Sensing there was no easy escape, instead of becoming more agitated or afraid, I became friendlier. Among the men was a woman who appeared to be ill. I asked her if she had gone to the doctor. Surprised, she opened up and began sharing her story. Soon, the others expressed curiosity about our conversation and began to relax their attitude toward me and my family.

I woke up with a clear sense of our shared humanity. I began to reflect on the common wounds we all share—and on practical solutions that I could be a part of. After all, the problem that had spurred my dream was not a "me" problem—it was an "us" problem that impacted all of the Americas. Narcotics trafficking has caused a great deal of harm to many countries in the world. However, through the gift of the dream, I was able to see beyond the traffickers' aggressive attitude and into their human shortcomings and broken hearts. The Wisdomkeeper has the tenacity to ground their actions in purposeful solutions. Rather than continuing to divide us further into factions of "me" versus "them," a tactic that is too commonly used by nearsighted politicians, the Wisdomkeeper has a vision of justice that holds every inhabitant of Earth in their clear and spacious heart.

Practice: Know Your Mountain

Reflect on the mountain that is your apu in this lifetime. For many people, this will be the mountain closest to their birthplace or the area where they grew up. If you did not grow up close to a mountain, you may sit in meditation and ask the question: "Which of the world's mountains is my guardian and protector?" Even if an answer to this question does not immediately come to you, be assured that it will arrive in its own time. You may also end up choosing an imaginary or mythical mountain, one that shows up for you and that you can feel but that might not even have a name.

It's important to recognize that every single one of us holds the archetype of the mountain within. In many cosmologies and spiritual traditions, the mountain is considered to be the home of the gods—the high perch from which all things are known and understood. Know that you can call on your mountain whenever you need to feel more grounded or when you are seeking protection and guidance. If you have chosen a physical mountain in the world and if it is possible for you, make a pilgrimage to honor your apu. You may get a sense from the apu of the kind of offering that would be most pleasing (such as tobacco, flowers, feathers, or something else). You may choose to burn your offering or to simply bury it in the mountain, to show your appreciation for its wisdom and tutelage.

Chapter 7:

THE EARTHKEEPER RITE

Never doubt that a small group of thoughtful, committed citizens can change the world. Indeed, it is the only thing that ever has.

— MARGARET MEAD

The Earthkeeper Rite, or Kurak Akuyek Karpay, connects us to a lineage of masters who hold the truest and most holistic vision of the meaning of life on Earth. They may not share scientific facts related to the evolution of our species or the kinds of innovations and technologies that are useful for our long-term flourishing. Rather, they sense the pulse of the life force that rumbles from the depths of our planet. Moreover, they have a bird's-eye view of the world that is similar to the perspective gifted to humanity after the photo titled *Blue Marble*—an image of Earth from 18,000 miles in space—was taken in 1972. The Earthkeeper has a vast and intricate awareness of our planet as one cohesive ecosystem—a single organism made up of many systems. (In the same year of the *Blue Marble* photo, biologist James Lovelock presented the Gaia hypothesis, showing Earth is a complex, self-regulating organism with many interconnected, co-evolving systems.) The Earthkeeper understands that we do not live on a lifeless rock full of disconnected beings and activities. Our wondrous Earth is constantly recycling and incubating new life.

Just as the Wisdomkeeper relates to the mountain and the Daykeeper to the fertile land, the Earthkeeper relates to the entire planet. The Earthkeeper's capacity for munay is enormous, with enough space to care for all beings on Earth. The more love they can hold, the greater their understanding of the interconnected systems of life and the fewer obstacles they encounter when taking whatever action is necessary in this moment.

Because Earth is part of a planetary and galactic system, the Earthkeeper contemplates the stars for inspiration and wisdom. One can imagine them gazing at the night sky, receiving the light that settles into their mind and hearts as pure knowing: a deep realization on the meaning of life. The task of the Earthkeeper is to translate heavenly wisdom and share it with others (one person, an entire village, or the whole of humanity) to inspire and guide in a holistic way.

Though the Earthkeeper has profound knowing, they are also at peace with not having the answers for everything . . . with resting quietly in the unknown. They honor the great mystery of the cosmos and trust that what they are meant to know will be revealed when the time is ripe. An Earthkeeper is comfortable in their own skin, as they master transforming their difficult or toxic emotions into clear vision and compassionate action. Like the ancient Taoist sages who viewed life as a river, an Earthkeeper knows when to swim against the current and when to surrender to the flow. Even when the path ahead is not clear, they recognize that the journey is as important as the destination.

While there are no age requirements to become an Earthkeeper (or to receive the wisdom of any of the lineages connected to the earlier rites), your age and life experiences (from deep pain and loss to exhilarating bliss) can offer a broader perspective and the benefit of multiple vantage points. As the poet Walt Whitman wrote, "I contain multitudes." Through every passing decade, we have an opportunity to shed our prejudices, to grow our wisdom and insight, to endure crisis and transformation, to nimbly navigate life's ups and downs, and to consider a variety of vantage points rather than clinging so tightly to our own.

This does not necessarily mean that age automatically equates to wisdom (many of us have met closed-minded older people who are "set in their ways" rather than entertaining greater tolerance and understanding), only that it is most common for an Earthkeeper to be an elder—in the sense that they may be both an "old soul" and someone who has gathered the experience of their biological years. Such a person tends to care for others, and the planet, in a way that is sincere and lighthearted. They can sense the urgency to attend to our world's most pressing problems and at the same time practice acceptance, understanding that all difficulties eventually pass and that the planet itself has lived through many cycles of birth and destruction. This understanding enables the Earthkeeper to be calm yet deliberate in their actions.

The Earthkeeper Rite is offered in the same way as the Daykeeper and Wisdomkeeper Rites in that the shaman balances the right and left sides of the body and taps on the initiate's head, heart, and belly, then transmits the connection to the lineage forehead to forehead. While the Daykeeper holds a torch for life to flourish on a daily basis, and the Wisdomkeeper can guide and inspire others to live out their purpose and take up the banner of a particular cause, the Earthkeeper is dedicated to bringing beauty and blessings to the whole world. This may not always look like social or political action, for it is not about how much an Earthkeeper literally does; it is about how much they can inspire others to make a difference. Just as an ancient Iroquois philosophy emphasizes the importance of making choices that result in a better world seven generations into the future, the Earthkeeper's prayers and ceremonies clear the path so that our children's children's children are able to reap the benefits of our service.

ORIGINS OF THE EARTHKEEPER RITE: THE POWER OF THE ELDERS

There is an enigmatic stone in Machu Picchu, near the path to access Huayna Picchu and the temple dedicated to the feminine power of Earth. Every day, visitors walk past it without recognizing the face of an Inka wearing a *chullo*, a traditional woven headdress, and gazing up at the Temple of the Sun. His cheek appears bulging with what must be a wad of coca leaves. Among the shamans who still venture into the City of Light of the Inka, he is called the *mascador de la coca*, the "one chewing the coca leaves." Coca leaves were available to people of all castes in the Inka Empire. But only the Inka could partake of the finest of the leaves, which were carefully harvested for the shamans and for royalty. Such a person is called the Kurak Akuyek. In Quechua, the word *kurak* means "elder" or "sage," and *akuy* means "to chew or masticate." Such a person "chews" higher wisdom so it can be delivered in an easy, discrete, and digestible manner—just as a mother condor chews food and places it into her baby's mouth. The Kurak Akuyek makes the mysterious wisdom and power of the cosmos digestible to those who seek mastery for the benefit of all beings.

As Alberto shares below, Don Manuel Quispe gave him this rite at the Temple of Moray, a gigantic set of concentric earthen rings in a valley near the city of Cusco; each level is lined with stone to form agricultural terraces and is where the Inka practiced a kind of genetic engineering and adapted their corn and other plants to the different ecological niches of the empire. The earth in the terraces was brought from each of the far corners of the Inka Empire to replicate the climate and growing conditions of that region.

> *"Here, the Inka crossbred their wisdom and their corn," Don Manuel explained. This was where his ancestors practiced an ancient form of biological engineering that resulted in more than 50 varieties of native corn and over 4,000 varieties of potatoes.*
>
> *"When you master the knowledge of seeds, you understand the wisdom of life seeking new forms of expressing the Divine," he continued.*

He then took his mesa and struck me on the head three times as well as on each shoulder and on my heart and belly.

When he finished, he blew into the crown of my head the "wisdom breath" of the generations of men and women before him who had committed themselves to the protection of Mother Earth and all her children. I felt a quiet warmth rush through my body, driving away the chill of the afternoon air.

"The Mother will look after you as you look after her; she will keep you healthy as you look after the health of all her creatures."

The Kurak Akuyek has achieved a balance in their three principal energetic centers: the belly, the place of llankay, or right action; the heart, the place of munay, or pure love; and the third eye, the place of yachay, or clear vision. They learned to perceive reality holistically and with equanimity, discovering the knowledge that is encoded in nature. Speaking the language of nature and of creation, they are able to change the weather, a person's destiny, and sometimes even the destiny of a village.

As vast as it is, the Earthkeeper's power is not ostentatious. On one occasion, when Alberto was still exploring the shamanic path as an anthropologist, he witnessed a *curandero* (a traditional healer) perform a healing, and he was fascinated by the performance: the curandero was shaking rattles, calling on the spirits, whistling and singing, and waving feathers in all directions. Later, Alberto had the opportunity to witness a very different expression of healing; an elder sat his patient a few feet in front of him and simply gazed softly at the patient for a few minutes. Alberto sat in anticipation of what was to come—surely, it would be another colorful display. Eventually, the healer raised his right hand and pointed his index and middle fingers at the patient's body. A few more minutes of stillness and silence . . . and the session was over. *Not very exciting for the camera*, Alberto thought.

The more wisdom and power a shaman has, the less they have to literally do. By cultivating ayni, a shaman can enlist the powers of nature to support their intention. In my experience, the most powerful medicine people are often the most humble, as they acknowledge that their gifts come through the grace of the

Great Spirit. In an Earthkeeper's prayers, they often say: "In the name of the Great Spirit and Mother Earth," or, "By the power of all the sacred mountains," or, "May the spirit of the waters heal my patient."

An Earthkeeper does not become haughty and drunk on the power that flows through them, for they understand that they themselves are not the source. Just as power was bestowed upon them, power can be taken away.

For 10 years I took groups of people to the jungles of Peru to work with a shaman who had great medicine. But then things shifted. During our group healing sessions, he began to fall asleep. At first, I assumed he was just tired, and I felt sorry for him so I gave him another chance. By the third time this happened, and after speaking with other people who worked with him, I realized he had lost his powers and was no longer able to lead a healing ceremony. As I later learned, this shaman had been crossing ethical boundaries and violating the trust of people who had come to see him. Due to his abuse of power, he was no longer infused with the auspices of the Great Spirit and Mother Earth. I prayed that he would be able to restore his ayni and return to his former passion of helping others with even greater devotion, care, and understanding.

OFFERINGS FOR THE WORLD

While writing this chapter, I went on a two-week pilgrimage to the Kingdom of Bhutan. Although I was fascinated with the beauty and sacredness that I was experiencing, my heart ached to see so many discarded plastic bottles along the trails. Thus, I suggested to the organizers of my tour that they could provide drinking water in a more ecological form. Moments later, I realized the problem was so much bigger than the country I was visiting: it plagues the entire world. My Earthkeeper spirit toned down my Daykeeper's limited perception so I could zoom out to see the big picture and not cast judgment on the people who were just trying to do their jobs and meant no harm.

Alberto shares a story of visiting the Peruvian Amazon in his early days as an anthropologist. During this time, he made friends in a remote village that hadn't been exposed to modern ways, and he communicated with the villagers through simple Spanish and lots of gestures. When Alberto asked them about the name of the river close to their village, they responded, "El río" (which translates to "the river"). He said, "Yes! I know it's the river, but what is its name?" After a few moments, Alberto understood that, for them, it was not necessary to name the river, since they did not venture very far from their village and the land around it. Nevertheless, as an exercise, Alberto drew with a stick in the wet sand a line representing the river they were familiar with, and then added other tributaries of the Amazon, until he'd given them an idea of how vast the entire river network was. The people of this village listened carefully and, sparked by curiosity, asked question after question until Alberto drew the outline of the Amazon River leading into the Atlantic Ocean. At this point, most of them were satisfied, but a couple of them wanted to know more, and Alberto gave them a sense of the many continents and oceans of the entire planet.

Such curiosity, vision, and regard for the entire planet is a sign of germinating the seed of the Earthkeeper. But even if this seed has not been awakened through such qualities, the Munay-Ki transmission will work to stir the seed's potential, and for someone whose seed has already awakened, the rite will serve to empower it.

The expansive vision of the Earthkeeper allows for the kind of outrageous creativity that the Earth itself displays as it births countless beings of extraordinary shapes and colors. The Earthkeeper contemplates the miracle of life joyfully while listening to the voice of Mother Nature, and they share with others the obvious and subtle ways of ayni.

Like the Daykeeper and Wisdomkeeper, the Earthkeeper has transcended the limited "me" so they can ground and center in the transpersonal "we." However, there are differences in these levels. Let's use the example of planting a tree. When we are living from the level of the healer, we might plant a tree to put our hands in the soil and feel more rooted on the earth; our vision might be that one day we may find comfort in hugging this tree. When living as a Daykeeper, we might plant a tree for the children who will be able to play under the tree or climb its branches and take its fruits. We might also be thinking about the elder who can rest in the shade offered by the tree. In this way, we dedicate the tree to the community.

From the perspective of the Wisdomkeeper, perhaps we plant the tree because we realize we need to reforest our region for the benefit of all creatures who live there. We may not have the resources to plant 2,000, 5,000, or 10,000 trees, but in planting one tree, we affirm, "I'm part of the solution." From the Earthkeeper perspective, we plant a tree for the benefit of the entire Earth. We do our part to make the planet healthier for the sake of all living beings, for seven generations and beyond.

Again, it is not so much about the literal quantity of things we do (which depends on our resources), but about our feelings and vision while doing it. It is not necessarily better to act from the perspective of an Earthkeeper than it is a Daykeeper; for example, there are people dedicated to planetary change who have unresolved issues with their family or community. In fact, their far-reaching "wisdom" might be a way to avoid what is happening in their immediate surroundings. They make themselves busy as an excuse not to deal with challenging matters at home. In the same way, someone might be so committed to their vision for the community, trying to fix "out there" what in reality needs to be tended within, from the perspective of the healer. In terms of the tasks and call to action that arise from the Munay-Ki Rites, it is important to remember that all of them serve an important purpose for our growth and development, and there is no hierarchy. The Munay-Ki as a whole bring us into greater harmony with ourselves, the Great Spirit, Pachamama, and all creation.

The benefit of attaining an Earthkeeper perspective is that, when we affirm our commitment to all life on Earth, we find exciting and creative ways of honoring the planet and all our relations.

We learn to embody what we long for (peace, health, beauty, and so on), and the more we embody, the more we inspire others.

With a holistic perspective, the Earthkeeper perceives beyond their backyard and their village and even the times they are living in. They are tuned in to the power and wisdom inherent in understanding larger cycles. An Earthkeeper is interested in the seasons and the cycles of the stars, and even of the cooling and warming of Earth, that mark the larger experience of life on this planet and tell a story that is much grander in scope. The Earthkeeper recognizes Earth's journey through the solar system and beyond, harnessing an awareness of how the planets, the sun, and the moon affect life on Earth. It is a great vision, but one that is grounded in humility.

The Earthkeeper connects with luminous beings in the invisible world that are said to be as tall as trees because their munay is so large. When we experience so much love, we too may connect to these beings, whom Alberto regards as archangels. Their stature is symbolic of their enormous wisdom—their far-reaching minds, hearts, and spirits. I have seen such beings in my dreams. I once dreamed of a being as tall as a building, who was shooting a basketball toward a giant basketball hoop. In the symbolic language of dreams, I knew he was shooting for a destiny that is healthier for Earth and all its inhabitants.

If you wish to carry the gifts of the Earthkeeper, it requires perceiving with clarity (yachay), feeling with an open heart (munay), and acting with impeccable honor (llankay). Holding the gifts of the Earthkeeper is not about assuming the weight of the world on your shoulders like Atlas—you can dedicate anything you do to all your relations, meaning all sentient beings, not just your friends and family.

As you learn to perceive from the vantage point of an Earthkeeper, consider what you value through your actions, feelings, and thoughts. How do you wield power and influence? Whom do you strive to benefit—a limited few or the many, including people, animals, plants, and other beings beyond your immediate environment? How big is your love?

THE TRUE CITIZEN OF THE WORLD

At some point, I heard a man say, "I am a citizen of the world. I often travel to different countries."

I said, "Really?"

"Yes, I'm in Europe, Asia, the United States, the Pacific Islands." He seemed very proud of his travels.

I felt the Earthkeeper in me perk up its ears. "When you go to all these places, what do you offer to the children you meet? What do you give to the homeless on the street? Or the people who are ignorant and need to learn something? Or the land, or the animals that perhaps need more space, having been pushed out of their habitats? What do you have to offer as you go around the world?"

He was taken aback, because he hadn't stopped to consider that perhaps he had a responsibility to give something to the people and places where he traveled—not only having as much fun, pleasure, and joy as he could. From the perspective of the Earthkeeper, the true citizen of the world feels the hunger of all children, or those disenfranchised by war, or the people who valiantly fight for their freedom in repressive states, or the Indigenous people who suffer on a reservation in the United States after having their traditional ways of life taken from them. The true citizen of the world sees that suffering exists at all echelons and becomes part of the solution. The true citizen of the world is an Earthkeeper.

However, the Earthkeeper's attention is not focused only on the tragic events that show that suffering is so present on our planet. The Earthkeeper also senses the beauty and aliveness that flourishes in all places—the good news, the children who play with abandon even in the most precarious conditions, the enthusiasm of people who find solutions to bring fresh water to faraway villages, and the ones who generate opportunities for children to study and for women to be appreciated in their work.

It is a gift to be with an Earthkeeper who knows how to bring us practical yet far-reaching messages of personal and planetary evolution. They don't place themselves on a pedestal or boast about all the important people they know and how much money they have. They know how to be human, and they are not attached to labels that might give them a sense of importance (such as the notion of being a "citizen of the world" who travels to exotic destinations). This is because they recognize the infinite spirit that acts through them, as them. They know who they truly are beneath the appearance they wear.

ONE PART OF A MAGNIFICENT PULSE

We may feel saddened by the state of the world and at a loss as to how "little me" can contribute to elevating the consciousness of humanity. Little do we recognize that such a sense of despair and helplessness only perpetuates the suffering we experience. One of my colleagues, Elise, who is a teacher of the Munay-Ki Rites, shares her story below. One of the most important things she discovered is that being passionate about social justice and caring for the welfare of humanity and the world need not emerge from a sense of conflict—as if we have to "fight" an imagined enemy in order to prevail. When we recognize our connection to all living beings, we stop separating the world into friends and foes; rather, we realize that we are one part of the magnificent pulse that runs through all creation. And by stepping into our authentic selves, we each have an important part to play.

> I was born in Germany within a cultural time that to me felt emotionally frozen, where personal feelings were either ignored or made insignificant due to the great shame of World War II—as though, because of that trauma, we weren't allowed to feel. As a child, I didn't understand this; I just felt I needed to be self-sufficient and never trust anyone.
>
> During my first class of the Four Winds Medicine Wheel, I received an illumination from another student. She leaned over me, asking, "What are you angry about?" over and over, insistently. It felt like she'd found a hidden ember within me. Her words stoked the flame until it grew bigger and bigger—until rage took over my body, and I felt lifetimes of human existence scream through me. The overwhelming responsibility of all trauma experienced by humanity throughout time engulfed me, as if I had been everyone all at once.

When I felt this, that we were truly one, I was consumed by a fire of all emotions—fury, grief, shame, innocence, passion, ecstasy—I was beyond this single little speck of life called "Elise." I didn't know it then, but that was the beginning of my understanding of what it is to walk as a Kurak Akuyek.

I am a poet. Before being initiated into the Kurak Akuyek, I ranted at open mic nights about social and political injustices, about whatever upset me and what I felt should be upsetting others, to encourage them to make changes. My unmoderated rage roared through me.

After receiving the seeds of the Kurak Akuyek, I felt a deep responsibility to share solutions through my poetry, to share visions and transmissions of our interconnectedness and the essence of love that we are, to invite the receivers into the embrace of unity awareness—and ultimately, to inspire them to be the transformation that they dream of for themselves and their families, communities, and planet.

Years later, as I prepared to lead that same first class as a teacher, I pleaded with the lineage for support; I asked them to speak through me, to guide me for the benefit of the students and the whole Earth. As I began to teach, I felt my heart expand throughout the room, as if I was becoming part of a constellation, every star of every person connecting. A power moved through my body, lifted above our room and into the sky: a vast river of what I can only describe as love.

Before these experiences, I thought more (and less) of myself and others. Before, I judged my inabilities or others' actions that didn't match my values as though we were separate from each other and I was separate from being enough. Although I was practicing various paths to expanding compassion and mindfulness, I felt driven by an undercurrent of pressure to "be better" or somehow prove myself. Looking back, I never would have attained it, as I kept raising the bar with every accomplishment.

After tasting unified consciousness, it is impossible to judge someone or some aspect of life without feeling the reflection internally. It is impossible to feel alone; it is impossible to feel there is such a thing as "wrong." This brings much into perspective and into daily choices involving not only oneself but compassion for others, and connection to this precious planet, to the cycles of everything.

We are light. We are the stars that ignite our collective waking dream, gifts for one another to return home, to love, with respect for all that is. Once this is realized, it can't be undone. Once this is realized, we *recognize each other, we trust each other, we trust life. From here, our choices are naturally generated on behalf of what is sustainable, beneficial, and fulfilling for All—or at least, to the degree possible within our ability with a global intent. We see we are just one part of a magnificent pulse that breathes us All.*

HEALING OUR WORLD

The Nguni people of Southern Africa have a philosophy that is known as *ubuntu*, which translates to "I am because we are." This statement reflects a trust in a universal bond that connects all living beings, and it is an inherently Indigenous perspective. However, even though every person on this planet comes from Indigenous roots, at some point, most Westerners have forgotten their connection, and eventually they feel rootless and bereft of hope. Modern living boasts all manner of creature comforts and technological conveniences but seldom the connection that we yearn for. In this sense, we have much to remember from the native peoples who never abandoned their intimacy with the spirit and the land that provides everything for their livelihood.

Alberto was blessed to receive the Munay-Ki from an Earthkeeper who understood the importance of sharing the wisdom from his tradition with Western seekers. Don Manuel said that Alberto's students should be the new caretakers of Earth and take responsibility and collective action for the betterment of the world.

Earthkeepers are those who have embarked on a journey of healing all their relations, within and without, as a way to embody a life-affirming and collaborative attitude toward the healing of the world, rather than having a contentious one.

The story of humanity is filled with monstrous war and suffering and with astonishing beauty and kindness. The Earthkeeper recognizes how legacies of both sides are passed down, from generation to generation, and how important it is to always strive toward ayni, reciprocity with all our relations. This means that repair needs to happen where there has been abuse and pain.

Regardless of background, the Earthkeeper rises above all conflict to find common ground, which in reality is planet Earth.

The Earthkeeper doesn't turn away, saying, "It's not my problem," or "I did not commit the crime," but is concerned for all those who suffer—people, animals, plants, and all earthly beings. They always remember that *I am because we are.*

For those of us who feel disconnected from our roots and the life force of the planet, it is time to remember how to celebrate our Indigeneity and to have deep respect for Mother Nature and her great generosity. The Earthkeeper understands that it is a gift to be alive on this planet—so that we can not only experience the abundance of this Earth but also meet deep suffering with fierce love. We have an opportunity to cooperate, with the understanding that each of us is a significant part of the whole. It is time to come together as Earthkeepers from all walks of life and to share our medicine so that it can be of benefit to all.

We must end disempowering personal stories and write new stories that resacralize Earth. For if we don't come together with all our relations, all life on the planet, we will not survive this pachakuti—this evolutionary opportunity for the death of who we used to be and the birth of the promise this world still holds for all of us.

Practice: Take Your Place on This Earth

The Earthkeeper Rite is connected to our desire to address the world's problems and sufferings. Find a peaceful place in nature or create a sacred moment at home. Place your hands over your heart and take a few deep breaths. Once you feel ready, sense the state of the world and ask, What are the things that most break my heart? Instead of shutting down your heart to not feel pain, allow yourself to be present with any discomfort. The idea is that you let your heart be "broken open" so your deep feelings can flow.

Often, we close our hearts to avoid feeling this pain because we think we are too small to make a difference. Instead, let your discomfort become a motivation to be part of the solution. In the spirit of the Earthkeeper, commit to helping a cause. Remember that there is an entire lineage of awakened souls that are equally committed, so you are not alone. The more of us who say yes, the stronger we are. You can build your ayni by doing your part.

Now that you have committed to being part of the solution through the power of your love, think in practical terms. What can you do about it? Some examples of how to contribute are to volunteer for an organization, such as a shelter for survivors of domestic violence or a prison full of inmates who long to be seen and heard, or to donate money to an organization that is working to support a cause you believe in. You can also choose to inspire others to get involved in the betterment of the world on a larger scale. For example, you could spearhead a movement within your workplace, school, or community by shedding light on a particular cause and identifying ways for everyone to contribute. The children of the future are already grateful!

Chapter 8:

THE
STARKEEPER RITE

Look up to the stars and not down at your feet.
Try to make sense of what you see, and wonder about
what makes the Universe exist. Be curious.

— STEPHEN HAWKING

In the early 1990s, the Starkeeper Rite, or Mosoq Karpay, was received for the first time during a ceremonial gathering of Andean shamans and Western practitioners at Mount Ausangate. This rite promised to liberate the initiate from their personal history and early life traumas in order to access the clean slate of their destiny as *Homo luminous.*

For Alberto, the Starkeeper Rite represented more than an individual initiation. It was also a collective cleansing designed to awaken the practitioner from the nightmare of Western history—an ablution that would prepare modern practitioners of shamanism to become agents of positive change during the great paradigm shift of the pachakuti.

The last pachakuti, as I mentioned earlier in this book, was said to have occurred 500 years ago, when the conquistadors lay siege to the Inka Empire and millions of Indigenous people died from smallpox the European invaders brought as the process of colonization began. The impact of the conquest rippled out for decades. Even today, the trauma of colonization is felt among the Indigenous communities who continue to defend their customs and territory from Western encroachment. The present pachakuti has already unleashed its waves of disruptive change, even as it takes time for the West to understand the scope of these changes that we are now experiencing.

After receiving the Starkeeper Rite, Alberto began lecturing and teaching about the impending Earth changes. He spoke about a great upheaval and how each of us could strive to become a beacon of light and hope in the rampant chaos—war, climatic challenges, and large migrations, among other threats. He inspired thousands of people to make changes in their lives, from the food they eat to the values they hold, and let them know that 2012 was the tipping point for the emergence of a new human, *Homo luminous*. That year, he became seriously ill, as he had become not only the messenger, but the message itself. He almost died as he crossed the threshold to a freer self that could heal and age differently. As a result of this experience, he wrote a guidebook for becoming the new human the prophecies speak about.

Before his health crisis in 2012, Alberto's message had focused on the dangers and difficulties of the great shift announced by the pachakuti. Like other contemporary voices, he spoke about the bloody and painful process that would accompany humanity's renewal. However, once on the other side of his own archetypal death and rebirth, the focus of his message curved greatly toward the good news about the coming of an era of great opportunity for humanity. Having survived his personal pachakuti, the know-how for embracing this great transformation grew in his own heart. To this day, he teaches that it is important to summon and embody peace and harmony on Earth, no matter how improbable it may seem. "The more people who envision a healthy destiny for life on Earth, the more juice we give to that possibility," he says.

I would add that when we join our hearts to that vision of peace and follow it up with courageous action, our dreams are birthed into reality. This is what the Munay-Ki is about: marshaling our potential to dream into manifesting the world we long for.

With the Starkeeper Rite, we are invited to stretch our perspective even further, beyond the scope of our blue-green planet so that we discover our intimate connection to the stars. We have already seen that the Earthkeeper Rite helped us view Earth as a member of the larger solar system. Now the invitation is to remember our place among the stars in our Milky Way Galaxy.

Though it may seem an outrageous idea to contemplate our relationship to the stars, it is a connection much more intimate than many of us can imagine. The first stars after the Big Bang produced hydrogen and helium, and the next generation of stars made carbon, magnesium, and nearly every element in the periodic table through a process known as *nucleosynthesis*. When stars die, nothing is wasted; similar to our Earth, which composts rotting matter, the next generation of stars is formed from the elements that remain after a star dies. And so, the cycle of life and death continues. Galactic evolution is responsible not only for stars but also for asteroids, planets, and the raw materials of life. As many of us know, we ourselves are made of stardust!

All ancient cultures looked to the stars for guidance; the Inka and their ancestors were also accomplished observers for how heavenly bodies moved. They developed a sophisticated astrology that guided the design of their Empire and indicated the times of offerings and ceremonies.

When we begin to remember this fundamental connection to the stars, our minds expand to consider greater cycles and eons of time. Since ancient times, sages have marked the great cycles that heralded the beginning and end of eras like a pachakuti or even larger chunks of time. For example, the marking of an end (and of a new beginning) on the year 2012 came more specifically from the Long Count dating system of the ancient Mayan calendar. They had calculated an astronomical cycle of 5,128 years beginning on their mythical creation date, which correlates to 3,114 BCE in the proleptic Gregorian calendar. Another example is a *kalpa* from the Hindu tradition, equivalent to 4.32 billion years and measuring cosmic cycles of existence (from golden ages to dark ages of not only humans but also interdimensional beings).

Observation of these eras of time enables us to see that everything comes to an inevitable end, and the cycle begins anew. Our perceptions are no longer limited to a specific name or gender in a human body in a particular nation, community, or era. Starkeepers are invited to consider the evolutionary process of humanity as part of a galactic event and are mindful of their impact on the future of our planet.

After receiving this rite, Alberto began speaking to students about the need to anchor ourselves beyond this time of great upheaval—and to begin to summon a desirable and sustainable destiny, allowing the future to guide us and pull us irresistibly toward a positive outcome for humanity within the ecosystems of the Earth. It's all too easy to succumb to hopelessness as we see the global impact of climate change, dysfunctional governments, and growing intolerance among people. However, Alberto's call, shared by other Starkeepers, is to "dream" an era of peace into existence, to know it as our destiny. In his words: "like a giant hand reaching [to us] from ten thousand years in the future and taking us into our collective destiny . . . a time when we would have transformed from *Homo sapiens to Homo luminous*."

This is a big invitation, to awaken a galactic consciousness, as many great ancient civilizations attempted. Specific individuals are also known for gazing out into space and time: cosmologists such as Claudius Ptolemy (2nd-century Greece) and Galileo Galilei (16th-century Italy), or more contemporary scientists like Albert Einstein and Stephen Hawking. They understood that the light from distant stars they saw through the eyepiece of their telescopes were from millions of years ago.

Starkeepers, attuned to the unraveling nature of the Galaxy, can catch a glimpse of our own human evolution. As enlightened minds from all times have done, we may receive wisdom—in the form of new codes—about our human destiny and about life beyond our human form. But we must attain an openness to the flow of existence that is much bigger than we have learned to contemplate.

On the day the Starkeeper Rite was received at Mount Ausangate, a new lineage was born—the lineage of the Starkeepers.

These are the ones who do not concern themselves merely with the exploration of space, but of time, with the aim of engaging more actively with our human destiny. These are the ones we are called to become.

On a personal note, I feel the seeds of all the other rites germinating within me and for the most part they are blooming in my life. With the Starkeeper Rite it is different. I can energetically sense the subtle threads connecting me to the stars, and I can observe in awe the mind-blowing magnificence of our galaxy. However, I feel like a baby as far as reaping the fruits of this transmission. So please take my words as inspiration and do not let them inhibit your own capacity to see through the veils of time and space.

ORIGINS OF THE STARKEEPER RITE: AN END AND A NEW BEGINNING

In Quechua, the word *mosoq* means "new." Thus, this rite was originally called *Mosoq Karpay*, or the "new initiation," and it is still referred to this way among the shamans of the Andes. When I asked Pascual (one of the Andean shamans we continue to work with) about the name, he explained, "It's the first time that this rite has appeared, and we haven't been given a name for it yet. But what is important is that now we're able to transmit it from person to person, and we no longer need to wait for lightning to strike or to have a luminous one come and seed us with this potential. Now, we can transmit it from mentor to pupil."

In 1989, Alberto's mentor, Don Manuel Quispe, recognized it was time to birth a new rite that could prepare humanity for weathering the challenges of the pachakuti. Alberto invited some of his students to join him at Ausangate. He'd expected five or so shamans to join them, but Don Manuel had assembled a large number of healers. More than a hundred men and women, with children and babies, showed up for the ceremony to receive the Mosoq Karpay, including renowned shamans like Mariano Apaza, Humberto Soncco, and Doña Bernardina Apaza. They were direct descendants of the Inka and dressed in ceremonial attire, and all had made the two-day pilgrimage to Ausangate.

When they met at the holy mountain, Alberto thanked Don Manuel for inviting him and his students: "What an honor to be received this way. Thank you for inviting us to be part of this amazing initiation."

Don Manuel replied, "I invited you because we needed someone to represent the conquistador, the white man. Our people need to heal the wound of the conquest. The raping of our mothers and kidnapping of our children. We need to bury the sword of the conquest."

Don Manuel paused and looked him in the eyes, and Alberto could see a tear running down his cheek.

"This rite is also for your people," he went on. "You and I are bringing it forth to the world. But neither of us is special—we are simply an instrument of our times."

For some initiates, this rite serves as a purification on a personal level. Among the shamans of the Andes, this initiation today is offered to prepare the student to receive other rites and further their subsequent training as a healer. The young shamans are beginning their training firmly anchored to a possible future free from the tragedies of the past. This rite begins the next level of their spiritual journey, where they can record their lessons onto a clean slate. Sometimes, the student is submerged in a sacred lagoon during the annual feast of Qoyllur Rit'i (the feast of the "snow star") near Mount Ausangate. This three-day festival celebrates the reappearance of the Pleiades constellation in their winter night sky and the coming of sowing seeds and later harvest (for this reason the Pleiades are called *qullqa* in Quechua, which means "storehouse"). The act of being submerged in the sacred waters is similar to a baptism or purification.

At a later time, depending on the initiate's maturity, they are offered the other rites, from healer (*Hampe*) to Earthkeeper (*Kurak Akuyek*). With each of these initiations, the medicine person will feel a stronger and irresistible call to accept their destiny at whatever level of development they have attained. If, for example, they are an Earthkeeper, they will become attuned to the greater cycles of humanity and Earth; if they are a Daykeeper, they will sense the responsibilities for their land and community.

For Alberto's students, including myself, this rite is an invitation to become an agent of transformation in these times of great change, as we anchor ourselves to a possible positive future. It takes us past the threshold of a now-obsolete worldview and to the dawn of the new time for humanity. In the Munay-Ki, the Starkeeper Rite is often given after the Earthkeeper Rite, so by the time the student receives this transmission, they are already steeped in the gifts and responsibilities of each level and can embrace this rite as an opportunity for the entire world and not just for their personal lives.

In my case, the Starkeeper Rite was the first of all the Munay-Ki Rites I received during my pilgrimage to Peru, as I relate in the "Beginning" section of this book. Now, 20 years after my first initiation by the Andean shamans, and with 17 years of experience guiding students on the adventure of the Munay-Ki Rites, I recognize that both the Andean and the Western path of the Starkeeper lead to a similar goal. When I am in ceremony with my paqo (Andean shaman) friends, and our awareness goes out to the stars, we find each other in the same timeless stream of consciousness, and we all know that it is a blessing to find the crack in the fabric of space-time and catch a glimpse of the golden era that lies ahead—and that, in some strange and mysterious way, is already here today.

NAVIGATING MULTIDIMENSIONAL TIME

The Starkeeper initiation opens us to a broader perception of our future, warning us about impending dangers and opportunities. It awakens within each of us the consciousness of avatars and prophets, the important agents of human transformation throughout history.

The Starkeeper recognizes that we have come to the end of the Western myth that Earth was created solely for our pleasure and exploitation. We're rudely awakened to the realization that we are living with an outdated and parasitic mythology that was crafted at a time when the Earth was still believed by many to be flat. We need a new mythology today—one that sweeps out to include the stars and planets and the symbiotic relationship of all life in the Universe.

The Munay-Ki Rites invite us to step out of ordinary time and into multidimensional time. Just as quantum physics describes the way space and time are intertwined, the ancients from the Quechuan Andes understood this and had a single word for it: *pacha*. To survive the pachakuti, the shamans knew that one had to go through the extremely narrow eye at the center of a torus that was infinitely small. A torus is a figure that is made when you rotate a closed curve, like a circle, around a line that is on the same plane but that does not cross it (like a donut with a narrow hole in its center, which is the shape of the Pi stone used for the Munay-Ki). In many ways, this concept is similar to a famous saying credited to Jesus: "It is easier for a camel to pass through the eye of a needle than for a rich man to enter the kingdom of God." (Luke 18:25) The wealth of the rich man represents the attachments that we form on this earthly plane. The gateway to the kingdom of God is similar to the eye of the needle, in that all humanity would have to transit through this extremely tight possibility, which is the birth canal for a new era. This means that you would have to squeeze through a passage so narrow that only your most essential self could possibly fit. You could bring none of your baggage—who you thought you were, including your name, title, gender, or financial status. Everything would have to be left behind, so your essence could flow forth into this new time, unencumbered by the baggage of the past.

In agreeing to be renewed in this way, we can "drop in between the moments," step outside of ordinary time, and "install" ourselves in an auspicious destiny, in the golden era of peace, so we can weather the storm of the pachakuti. The storm could last 10 months, 10 years, or 10 decades—whatever the case, the Starkeeper Rite equips us so that we can stay close to the eye of the storm and successfully undergo its tests and trials.

For the Q'ero, who were insulated from the effects of the Spanish conquest for centuries, the current pachakuti forced them out of the 16th century. They had been living in the mountains with no technology, no cell phones, no television, no factory-made clothing. At some point during the 20th century, they came down from their mountain, as they understood it was time to join the rest of the world. They had been living just as their ancestors lived a few centuries ago, and in a very short time, they stepped into the 20th century. They had to leap through 500 years of history in almost the blink of an eye.

Modern physics suggests that our perception of time is not absolute, and the laws of nature do not exclusively enforce a linear experience of time; indeed, many fundamental laws of physics are time-reversible, remaining valid in either direction of time's flow. During this era of planetary crisis, human evolution is no longer guided only by the old laws of Newtonian mechanics that suggest change is gradual and incremental, occurring over millennia, but by the laws of quantum physics, whereby evolution can occur very rapidly. Biologists call this process *quantum speciation* (or punctuated equilibrium); that is, in times of extraordinary crisis, such as the one through which we are living, new evolutionary traits can appear very quickly.

The shamans of the Andes understand that it is possible to break free from the bondage of linear time; it is possible to find the future of humanity through our star consciousness, to journey far into the future to find the wisdom of who we are becoming, and to bring this information into our energy fields today. The Starkeeper has the ability to break free from time itself, so they can tap into the wisdom of the past, or journey forward along the possible timelines of humanity to help steer the world toward peace, sustainability, health, and ayni with all nature.

Think of how you, like a Starkeeper, can be attuned not just to your own personal destiny, but to the collective journey of all humanity. Think of your own connection to the stars—the elements that make up your body and everything you see around you. Reach into the depths of your primeval consciousness, recognizing that you have been on a very long journey, and now it is possible to move faster than the speed of light toward a new awareness for the well-being of all life.

DEEP SPACE AND DEEP TIME

Modern science continues to affirm the magic and majesty of our cosmos. Today, the most powerful space observatory ever created, the James Webb Space Telescope, has taken us deeper into the cosmos than we've previously been able to see, revealing snapshots of galaxies that are billions of years old. Indeed, to gaze upon these images and into the reaches of space is to catch a glimpse of a faraway past. To see a star that is a million light years away is to see it as it was a million years ago, when light first streamed from its surface toward us.

In the neighborhood of the stars, we are mere babies—and there is much we could stand to learn from our celestial friends. One of my students, Steffen, who became a teacher of the Munay-Ki Rites, discovered his own connection to the lineage of the Starkeepers. The Inka are said to be the descendants of the star nations, specifically the Pleiades—and Steffen's encounter with the Starkeeper lineage helped him to forge a relationship with a reality beyond this earthly one.

> The energy of the Starkeepers came to me in a dream, long before I even knew what it was. I was in the beginning of my spiritual awakening— working my way out of decades of hardship, zigzagging to avoid others' judgment, stress-induced depression, childhood trauma, and a narrow life hemmed in by many forces. I lost my few loved ones early on, and for years after, I kept my mouth, my truth, and my heart shut, controlling my emotions to prevent being hurt again.
>
> In my dream, I fast-forwarded through my life, from my high-school graduation party to inner-work seminars many years later. Suddenly, I came to a majestic tree. In my dream, it appeared in the middle of the night: a soft, cool breeze raising goosebumps along my neck. A full moon shone in the crystal-clear sky. I felt I was waiting for something, but I didn't know what. Then, a group of fast-moving lights high in the skies

came toward me: beautiful, colorful lights that radiated energy. My heart began to pulse as I focused on the lights; with each breath, it felt like invisible hands were opening my heart space a bit more. Without warning, the lights descended right into my energy field, through my heart, then out of my body again, whispering, "We are the Pleiades; we have come to remind you of who you are becoming."

The seed was planted that night, and I began to nurture it without knowing what it would become.

A decade later, while studying with the Four Winds Society, I would learn that in the mythology of the [shamans] from the Andes, their people are descendants of the Pleiades. In my long-ago dream, the future reached out to draw me to a destiny in which I would be informed and guided by my future healed self instead of being pushed by my heritage and stories into a possibly dire future. Like a giant hand that reaches back in time from the future, the Mosoq Karpay informs us in the here and now, guiding us into our becoming.

By following that thread of energy that the light of the Mosoq had gifted me that night, I unconsciously invited synchronicities into my life. My life shifted, and linear time and three-dimensional space became but one perception of reality. This rite helped me feel the support of spirit and gave me the courage to finally open up my heart again, releasing all I have to share with the world and to embody more who I had been all along.

CULTIVATING COURAGE

Every rite of the Munay-Ki moves us more deeply into a transpersonal perspective. For many of my students, imagining themselves 10,000 years into the future is perhaps the ultimate transpersonal exercise, as the "self" being imagined is not the one we are used to seeing in the mirror. This body and everyone I know will be long gone 10,000 years from now, but I can go through the exercise of expanding my consciousness into an awareness of our future being. Because energy is neither created nor destroyed, meaning that the essence of what we are is infinite and so, too, is consciousness.

During the week when Alberto and his students received the Starkeeper Rite alongside the Q'ero, a group of shamans who "read" the prophecy spoke of the coming of a new age for humanity: a thousand years of peace, a "millennium of gold." This millennium of gold would not suddenly land in our laps. We would have to endure a difficult passage into this new era. The purpose of the Starkeeper Rite was to steward us safely through that storm. In facing any pachakuti, the first rule is to adapt and survive the times at hand. This does not mean that we must assimilate into systems that are cruel and unjust, but we must learn to adapt to the changes and weather the storm by being calm and becoming part of the solution—part of the seeding of the earth after the wind has died down.

The Starkeeper Rite helps us to realize that the paradigm we've been living is obsolete. We begin to see that we are being ushered into a future that bids us to step out of our comfort zone and predictability. In a time of such tremendous change, it is no longer sufficient to cling to our old plans, as comforting as they may have been. We must be willing to release, let go, and be open to the new paradigm—and to also co-create and be part of it. This is a process I have seen come to life countless times with students who are brought to the path of shamanism, usually after times of crisis that change their perspective forever and help them forge a new understanding of their purpose.

We are not only waiting for the prophecy to happen; we are the process for the prophecy coming to fruition.

The Starkeeper Rite created a new lineage of prophets, however—and I cannot emphasize this enough—receiving this rite does not automatically make someone a prophet. Instead, we become agents of the prophecy, intimately invested in our collective destiny and the change the world is screaming for.

How is any of this practical? For most people, contemplating anything beyond one's own life or even seven generations into the future may feel far removed from their day-to-day reality, especially if they are uncertain of what they'll do tomorrow to pay the bills and rent. However, it is possible to hold both the absolute and relative truths of existence. Dealing with our problems today doesn't mean that we stop being one with life in the cosmos—it just means that we may still have to figure out our lives on the level of the Healer Rite (for example, by healing our relationship to money), at the same time that we cultivate a more panoramic perspective.

To develop one's awareness at the Starkeeper level, it helps to have achieved a certain freedom from day-to-day burdens. I recall the days in which feeding my children and creating a warm home were my most important tasks. At that point, my priorities were at the level of the Daykeeper, until I felt an authentic calling to continue studying and traveling, organically cultivating the qualities of the Wisdomkeeper. Nowadays, although I spend a lot of time teaching and writing, as well as caring for my gardens, family, and community, I feel a responsibility to engage in contemplative practices. The seeds of my Starkeeper have begun to germinate as I develop my curiosity for what lies beyond our current phase of humanity, and even beyond my existence on this earthly plane.

Starkeeper awareness helps us realize how fleeting this lifetime is—how precious our own existence is, which is the blink of an eye in the larger scope of the galaxy. This can give us the necessary courage to act today, to move beyond our own selfish and time-bound interests. The Starkeeper Rite offers us an awareness that can teach us to reside in a higher perspective wherein we hold everything with both lightness and reverence, rather than taking ourselves so seriously. Just as with the Earthkeeper Rite, we are reminded not to sweat the small stuff, not to get trapped in nonsense drama, and to engage the bigger, more transcendental purpose.

Practice: Spark Your Relationship to the Stars

Just as ancient sages did, take time to look to the heavens and begin seeing life from a much vaster perspective. You may wish to purchase a telescope or a powerful set of binoculars that allows you to see the night sky in greater detail, especially if you live in an area where light pollution makes it difficult to see the stars.

When you feel ready, ask the skies which star or constellation will help you develop a Starkeeper's consciousness. For example, when I am in South America, I look for the Southern

Cross, which helps me to orient myself to where I am, physically and spiritually. In North America, I look to the Big Dipper. Whenever you have time or are in a place that allows you to, look up to the sky and find your guiding star. Over time, you will begin to learn your way around the heavens by locating that star. You will also begin to develop a dialogue with the heavens that helps you cultivate a deeper understanding of the natural world and humanity's place within it.

Chapter 9:

THE
CREATOR RITE

Imagine yourself sitting in a quiet place in nature,
being still and silent inside yourself.
Breathe in the power of the universe.
Breathe out the power of the universe.
Breathe in the love of the divine.
Breathe out the love of the divine.
Breathe in the light of the Absolute.
Breathe out the light of the Absolute.

As you inspire the power, love, and light of the universe, you
exhale sharing love and light with all living beings. As you breathe,
experience yourself expanding into the eternal light of all life. You
are not a separate entity, you are one with all that is.

Imagine.

— SANDRA INGERMAN, *MEDICINE FOR THE EARTH*

The Creator Rite, or Taitanchis Rantis Karpay, invites us to discover our infinite nature, which is inseparable from the Great Spirit and all of creation. It also leads us to assume stewardship for all creation—from the smallest grain of sand to the largest cluster of galaxies. You discover that the Great Spirit works not only through you but as you and that all of creation is not happening only around you but inside you. Stewardship of all things visible and invisible becomes natural and inevitable. The Creator Rite helps us realize that creating is not only a privilege but also a responsibility meant to be undertaken with our full yachay (right vision), munay (right love), and llankay (right action).

In Quechua, one translation of Taitanchis Rantis is "to be equivalent to the Creator," although for the purpose of the Munay-Ki it can very well mean "to be equivalent to the Creatrix." Thus, for the rest of this chapter please consider the word *Creator* as a gender-free noun. This rite helps us to recognize that we are not separate from the creative force that brings forth every living being. We are both the dark space where creation occurs and the light and sounds that it creates, the stillness and the dynamic movement of the elements, Earth, and the heavens. Additionally, we understand that creation happens in cycles of birth, maturation, decay, and death. We don't hold to the idea that what is created must last forever, because we know it will have an end. We don't mourn the changes in the same way we may have before, because we recognize we have everything that is necessary to continually dream new worlds into being. Even when we experience loss, we have something to look forward to.

The Creator Rite can help us quiet the mind of the little "me" who is hungry, tired, selfish, or afraid by helping us witness and feel the vastness of life. When we commune with that vastness, we transcend the daily toils that normally weigh us down. When our minds and perception are still, we see within ourselves the world that is all around us—as if we are a lake that reflects the trees, sky, stars, clouds, and everything else perfectly. This stillness helps us perceive everything around us and recognize that it is within us as well as outside of us. When we know we are one with all that is, we truly harness our ability to co-create.

There is an important distinction here: to be "as the Creator" is not the same as saying, "I am *the* Creator." This is too inflated a perception and does not fit our human experience. The stage of being *as* the Creator means one has all the elements of the

Creator, but they are fitted to their own stature. To understand this, consider the way a drop of water from the ocean contains the same components, molecules, atoms, and particles as the ocean, yet the drop of water is not the whole ocean. Likewise, we can acknowledge that we don't have control over the totality of existence. Everyone around us is a co-creator, just as we are, and when we are not awakened, we continue to create and experience hunger, jealousy, or any kind of drama.

Indeed, we are creating every single day—with every thought and intention. When we are aware of this, we can consciously choose which colors we're going to use to paint the day, the week, or our collective destiny.

ORIGINS OF THE CREATOR RITE: CALLING DOWN THE GREAT SPIRIT

Taita translates to "father" and *taitanchis* is "the Great Creator," as that Father who wants us to be well. *Rantis* means "to be like." So *Taitanchis Rantis* is the Quechua term for "to be like the Creator" or "to be as the Creator." The Taitanchis Rantis initiation was a joint adventure undertaken between Alberto and a group of Andean shamans, mainly Don Manuel.

One morning in January 2005, while we were living in Miami, Alberto and I walked a couple of blocks to the supermarket, and I noticed that he was quieter and more introverted than usual. So, on the way home, I asked what was going on.

He responded almost as if he were in a trance, "There is a ninth rite."

"What do you mean?" I asked, surprised.

"Don Manuel [who passed away in 2003] told me that after the Mosoq Karpay, there would be another rite, the Taitanchis Rantis, or Creator Rite . . . I didn't know when it would be ready, but now I feel the moment is ripe—the world needs this initiation. Altogether, the nine rites form the whole of the Munay-Ki."

It felt as if we were no longer in Miami but in a liminal space of new possibilities. For the first time I was hearing the phrase

Munay-Ki; until then the rites had been a collection of discrete rituals. By the time we put the groceries down on our kitchen counter, I had learned that the Munay-Ki would be this body of wisdom meant to offer a path to self-realization. Throughout the day, Alberto gave me hints about the plans that were shaping in his mind so that he could gather the shamans required to bring the rite from the heavens to Earth. Just like with the Mosoq Karpay, this would involve a pilgrimage to Mount Ausangate in the company of some of the most accomplished medicine people of the Andes.

Seven months later, in July 2005, we found ourselves praying at the feet of Mount Ausangate. We had made offerings to the mountain in the days prior so that we could be allowed to enter its most sacred inner spaces, which is not always visible to ordinary eyes. Six senior shamans were by Alberto's side, making the offerings and saying the prayers in Quechua, asking the Great Spirit for the Taitanchis Rantis to come and help humans create the new world beyond the great upheaval.

I sat on one side of the shamans while 20 Four Winds graduates completed the circle. That morning, the skies were a beautiful blue canopy above us, and the glaciers sparkled under a blinding sun. However, soon after the prayers began, clouds gathered over us, and lightning struck nearby. No more than a half an hour later, as the shamans offered their kintus, thick gray clouds pelted us with hail. We immediately recognized that the new rite was being showered upon us by the lightning that was now striking 200 yards away. The hail was so large and fast that we had to run into our dining tent to protect ourselves. We were all convinced that the heavens had responded to our request.

Three months later, Alberto and I held the first Munay-Ki training. With the help of four shamans—Don Humberto Soncco, Doña Bernardina Apaza, Don Francisco Chura, and Don Pascual Apaza—we offered the nine rites to 150 students of the Four Winds Society within a single week. These students hailed from all over the world, and when they traveled home, the rites returned with them. From that moment, the seeds of the Munay-Ki began to span the globe; soon, thousands of Western practitioners were sharing the blessing with others.

Just like with the previous rites, the person giving the transmission touches the right and left sides of the body (solar/masculine and lunar/feminine) to create balance; and then taps on the initiate's head, heart, and belly to bring coherence between the three centers. This is followed by the actual transmission of the lineage—forehead to forehead.

The Q'ero and Western shamanic practitioners alike use this rite to anchor themselves in the time beyond the great crisis of the *pachakuti*—in the new era of peace we are committed to embodying. We all see the need for clean water, fresh air, healthy food, and collaboration rather than divisiveness. The details may look different for each of our communities, but at the level of the Creator, we can agree about what the world needs for humanity and all other species to thrive.

The attitude of the Creator is not exclusive to the Munay-Ki. Anyone with a degree of awareness can recognize another fellow human with the same openness of heart, clarity of vision, and courage to act. In the spiritual realm, the awareness of such highly awakened people unites them so that it is a singular force guiding the world toward goodness. Thus, while there are specific lineages for each Munay-Ki Rite, there is a link to a common lineage that steers all traditions to the plan of the Creator who wants us to be well.

This sense of oneness can be found in our work with those Andean shamans who have been an integral part of initiating Westerners into the wisdom of the Munay-Ki. Together, we travel to offer the rites, and we understand each other without having to say very much. We are united by a common purpose, and the differences in our words, attire, and customs do not matter. There is a deep understanding between us that we are showing up for the healing and fulfilling of our shared destiny on this planet.

THE SAME BUT DIFFERENT

It is important to recognize that while the Creator Rite brings us to the level encompassing everything in creation—including our cosmos and all other universes and dimensions that may exist—the experience of unity does not negate the reality of being human on planet Earth. We are not being asked to throw everything into a blender until we are reduced to an undifferentiated primal soup. The Universe is filled with galaxies, stars, planets, and life forms, all of which are distinct from one another. Our unitive consciousness holds this paradox: a single force throbs throughout all creation, animating everything with purpose; however, this oneness encompasses infinite shapes and qualities. We are the same in that we share the elements and consciousness that create us (we all share hydrogen and carbon and other elements), but each individual is a unique dance of these building blocks.

The Creator Rite helps us to appreciate the infinite forms that the Great Spirit is continually dreaming into existence. Some of us are more and some of us are less awakened to this multidimensionality. It also helps us maintain a sense of "right size," so we do not mistake ourselves as being the next avatar, prophet, or "chosen one." We have the same *munay* as the Great Spirit but must navigate life as a human in a finite form. With the blessing of the Creator Rite, we learn that both of these components—the infinite and the earthly—are part of one complementary whole.

Throughout the years of teaching shamanic practices and offering the rites, I have witnessed my students evolving. During the first couple of days when we sing together around a fire, there are always a few individuals who want to proclaim to the group their uniqueness; instead of chanting in the same tone, which creates a sense of cohesion, they sing in a totally different key, which causes chaos and confusion. But as the participants move through the process of healing, and by the time they've received the Creator Rite, the chant becomes harmonious. When people are no longer wrapped up in the drama of their individual stories, they can shine effortlessly without trying so hard to stand out.

It is similar to the way an orchestra works. Every instrument is necessary for creating a symphony. There may be moments when it is appropriate to highlight some instruments or a single player, but the music is much more than the sum of its individual parts. Likewise, we can learn to be who we are in the world without turning it into a one-person show or competition; we do not need to drown out other voices or be drowned out in return. We can hold the "both/and" of our individuality and oneness with grace, recognizing that life would be so much less interesting without the dynamic tension that exists between seeming opposites.

BREAKING THE SPELL OF POWERLESSNESS

Many people walk through life in a daze, not recognizing that they are co-creating every moment of their day, from how they are spending their rest time to the kind of work they are doing. They feel they are victims of their routine—as if they have no power over their circumstances. For too many people, this is a spell that never gets broken. Day in and day out, they are taken in by the trance of this temporal dream; they believe that the role they play, the role they have unconsciously chosen, is more real than anything else.

When we receive the Creator Rite, we learn to break the spell. We realize that we have the power to generate the awareness that will allow us to feel a sense of flow and connection and experience the joy and wonder of being alive in a world that is constantly being cultivated anew.

One of my students, Martina, discovered the joy of nurturing the seed of the Creator Rite. She found that when we awaken to who we truly are—powerful co-creators with the Great Spirit—we learn to relish the beauty and grace of every waking moment. Our entire life becomes our art. Martina shares:

For 15 years, I worked in the banking industry in high-demand positions. Every single day, I tried to do everything in the best way, putting all my energy and effort into being completely in service to people and institutions. When I became the mother of two beautiful boys, I got the brief chance to remember the wonder of life. But soon, the business world snatched me up again, so I danced painfully between these worlds, doing my best for everyone around me.

Living this way was unsustainable; step by step, I lost a sense of my own inner wishes, my humor, my joy. In the end, I lost myself. My body tried to warn me, but I ignored these signs and my soul's whisper to change my life. Sadness spread like a dark shadow I tried to hide from everyone, even from myself. One day, my sister saw me and said, "You need to find your inner light again, and we can do this by starting on the energetic level."

When I received the Munay-Ki Rites, especially the Taitanchis Rantis, for the first time, my soul was deeply touched, and my heart whispered gently, "Here and now, I'm coming home." This rite shifted all my intellectual, acquired knowledge deeply into my heart to let me feel who I really am. Suddenly, I saw and sensed nature around me pulsing with vibrant energy: in every tree, every dewdrop, in birdsong, in the soft breeze of the wind. I enjoyed silence more and more and searched for this sacred space around and within.

After receiving the rites, when I kissed my sleeping children, my senses were awake to the full experience: their hair brushing against my nose, the smell of their skin swirling around me. In response to the wonder of life, deep, unconditional love blossomed in my heart. It is such a privilege to be here on this beautiful Earth and to live consciously from the bottom of my heart.

Now I know that life is not about doing everything perfectly for everyone; it is about being completely me in this world. This rite guided me to see that all I long for is already here; it is up to me to realize this. This sacred essence inside can never be completed by anything from the outer world. No kind word can really increase it, and no critical word can ever diminish it. My light-filled being is already whole and infinite.

The Munay-Ki Rites encouraged me to remember the magic of life and to see the pulsing life force in everything. They taught me to turn my believing into a deep knowing that I can be protected every single moment of my journey.

THE PERMEABLE ME

The Munay-Ki Rites teach us how to live a healthy, embodied life, and as we progress through the rites, we begin to perceive from a much larger perspective. We are invited to make ourselves permeable so that we can breathe in the flowers and trees, hear the birdsong and the cries of the children, and take in the entirety of this world with both its beauty and its pain. The reason for becoming permeable is not to absorb the burden of everyone's suffering but to experience life more fully and deeply. As we do this, we can see and feel the joy and terror that are integral aspects of this earthly plane.

When we connect with the Healer and Daykeeper lineages, we are given tools that help us to recycle heavy energies and painful emotions. Now, at the level of the Creator, we recognize that our breath is connected to everyone else's breath—including the rich and the poor, the healthy and the ill, the babies and the elders, those who are relishing orgasmic joy, those who are contorted in the agony of physical and spiritual pain, those who languish in loneliness and despair, and those who are in the midst of a great awakening.

When we are able to hold this complexity, we come to dream the world into being in a much richer way. It is like adding hues to your artistic palette so that you can create with greater vibrancy. This means perceiving the world through a more holistic and inclusive lens and allowing our limiting ego identification to temporarily disappear; in this way, we can enter new perspectives and transcend our narrow beliefs to entertain the deeper layers of existence.

This is the way of the Creator Rite. As the artist of our perceptions, we sustain and nourish our creations, maintain them over time until they ripen and bear fruit, and finally let them die, decay, decompose, and return to the Great All so they can become compost for new creativity and new life.

The Creator Rite instills a strong sense of our interdependence so we recognize that the goal of acting purposefully in the world is not to eradicate what we do not like; it is to bring balance to a disharmonious world. Most of us, whether we are on a spiritual path or not, recognize that there are too many forces bringing harm and destruction to humanity and all nature. This is why we need more awakened creators who are dedicated to restoring a healthy balance and to bringing more joy and beauty into our world. There is a place for everything in the Universe, but there are patterns that need to die in our world so that we can co-create with the munay of the Great Spirit the golden millennium of peace.

Practice: Embrace the Creative Process

To be effective Creators in our own lives, we must recognize that a creative process is not simply about the act of birthing; it is also about sustaining what we create and destroying or releasing it when and if it is time to make space for something new.

For this practice, I recommend that you write the answers to the following questions. In addition, you may want to blow your answers into seeds, symbols, or stones that you can then place somewhere special, like on an altar or somewhere auspicious in nature. (Seeds for what you want to create, a symbol for that which you need to sustain, and stones for that which you are releasing.)

1. What am I longing to create in my life and for the world? (It is generally easiest to choose one thing, such as a supportive partnership, a beautiful sanctuary to call your home, or a new career.)

2. What practical steps do I need to take to create what I want?

Take a moment to transition and then continue with these two questions:

1. What have I created that I need to put more time into sustaining (for example, a business, a creative project, or a community initiative)?

2. What are the best ways I can direct my energy toward sustaining that which I have already created?

Again, take a few calming breaths to transition, and ask yourself these last questions:

1. What is obsolete in my life and is blocking my energy to create anew (for example, an out-of-sync relationship, a dead-end job, a bad habit that is dragging you down, or anything else that might be making it difficult to manifest what you most wish for)?

2. In the past, is there anything I have let go of that ended up liberating my energy so that I could direct it toward something that served me and others well?

It is not always easy to let go of things that no longer serve us. Often, we can be reluctant, as it was once a source of joy for us. The prospect of letting go can bring up fear, grief, and scarcity. We might wonder, *What if I don't find anything better?*

However, letting go is an integral aspect of the creative process. We must make space for new possibilities—and trust that opportunities will grace our lives when we take that leap of faith into the unknown.

If you are finding it difficult to let go, if you still have a strong emotional attachment, allow yourself time and space to grieve. You may wish to dance, stomp, or weep your grief. You may also journal about your feelings and invite guidance from the Creator lineage. Finally, you can actively visualize the new life that will emerge once you are able to release what no longer serves you.

Remember that death is an active part of the creative process. As we release what is ready to be banished, this liberates energy to sow the seeds we wish to grow for the future.

Chapter 10:

THE RITE OF
THE WOMB

It is my prayer that together we will welcome the wisdom of women
back into the collective field, where it may help to transform the
human family and heal the ravaged earth.

— MIRABAI STARR, *WILD MERCY*

The Rite of the Womb, or Kisma Karpay, is the tenth and final transmission of the Munay-Ki Rites, and it connects us to the mysteries of the feminine. While masculine spiritual traditions emphasize "rising" to the heavens and scaling the highest peaks toward the light, the feminine practices are quests of incubation. They prompt the seeker to find refuge in womb-like spaces, where we may have to adjust our eyes to the dimness of the light and grow more comfortable with surrender.

Sometime in 2002, I had a dream that I would only begin to understand three years later. In the dream, I was six months pregnant, but I knew that my baby was no longer alive. I attempted to balance on a skateboard, careening down a winding road that ended in a dense jungle. As I approached the green canopy, guerrilla fighters shot at each other from behind trees. My heart racing, I finally arrived on level ground. Here, four women appeared dressed in diaphanous gowns, and they urged me to quickly follow them into a little cabin. They explained, "We are your midwives, and we are going to help you deliver your dead baby." Comforted by their warmth and wisdom, I agreed to their help. I followed them to a cozy room in the back where there was a fluffy bed enveloped by veils. I lay down in total trust, and just when I had begun to relax—bang! I heard such a loud gunshot, I was startled awake.

This dream would haunt me for many weeks. In early 2005, while I was cleaning my bedroom shelves, my old journal fell to the floor and opened to the page where I'd recorded that dream. At the end of the passage, I'd written, "I cannot imagine what this means." At the time, as I stood reading it, I thought to myself, *I still don't have a clue what this means!*

That afternoon, I experienced an episode of posttraumatic stress as I collapsed into my old fears. While the world around me turned black and the demons in my head spoke in loud voices, my instinct was to curl into a fetal position to protect myself. It was cold outside, so I lay on a warm carpet close to the fireplace. Just then, as I was lulled into a semi-trance, the women in diaphanous gowns who'd appeared in my dream burst into my awareness. "Marcela! Marcela! Come closer to the fire," I heard them say. "We are the midwives who have been waiting to help you give birth to your dead baby."

As I heard their words, I finally understood. I knew what the women were referring to. I was carrying death. I was literally pregnant with death. I had been storing in my womb all the terror I had felt throughout my life—it was the perfect container. The uterus can hold visceral memories from our past, containing unconscious beliefs, patterns, and anything that must be brought to our awareness to be healed.

Together, the women and I completed the process that had been cut short by the sound of gunfire in my dream. Both my hands and theirs pushed a wad of fear and death out through my birth canal and fed it to the flaming fire. By now, I had gone into a deep trance and my entire body began to tingle. I could now see and understand my situation. For years of being overly dependent on my ex-husband and allowing him to treat me poorly, all in exchange for security, I had given away my power. This was the same pattern lived by my mother, her mother, and many generations of women before me. It was time now to reclaim my power and protect my life force.

Two years earlier, I had been in Peru receiving my first Munay-Ki initiation, the Mosoq Karpay. My life had been turned upside down when I had left my marriage and had to find a new home for myself and my children, and my emotions and physical body felt raw, as if I had just barely made it through the portal that marked the beginning of my transformation.

Tears of gratitude streamed down my cheeks as flowers showered down upon me from the spirit world and more women appeared, dancing in colorful dresses. "We are a lineage of women who freed themselves from suffering . . . and we have come to teach you to do the same," they said with great love.

The journey continued as I was transported to a warm and dark cave—a womb-like place—and they invited me to dance with them. "This is your initiation into our lineage, Marcela!" they sang. "We will be by your side."

I wrote in detail about this initiation in my book *Awakening Your Inner Shaman*. Now I can share where this story eventually took me.

ORIGINS OF THE RITE OF THE WOMB: EASING SUFFERING TO BIRTH NEW CREATIONS

In 2014, while I was leading a group of women to work with plant medicine in the jungles of Peru, I met the lineage of women once more. It was during a nighttime ceremony, shortly after I'd ingested the psychedelic brew—a traditionally prepared ayahuasca and chacruna concoction. The midwives appeared and informed me, "Marcela, you are called now to offer our blessing to other women. We are going to give you a transmission."

The space around me turned into a laboratory surrounded by flasks that were fermenting green juices from jungle plants. The lineage had carefully chosen certain specimens of plants to inject into my body, concentrating on my womb. They said, "The jungle is full of life, and we need to infuse you with this life force." They explained that in both my own experiences and in the world at large, we've been recruited into a cult of death and illness. "We need to bring you back to life, and you're going to offer our message to the world," they declared.

I could see the neon-green liquid coursing through my veins and arriving at my womb, clearing every cell until there were no dense energies left—nothing toxic, only pristine greenness. The midwives said, "The womb is not a place to store fear or pain; it is for creating and giving birth to life."

They had offered the Rite of the Womb to me, a blessing I was meant to share with other women. "For all life comes from the womb," they informed me. "This rite will also heal men and help to change the world."

It all made sense to me. But despite the powerful transmission I'd received, doubts crept in when the midwives explained that the Rite of the Womb should be one of the Munay-Ki Rites.

"Who will believe me?" I asked. "Who am *I* to share this message with others?"

"Alberto delivered the rites of the Munay-Ki to the modern world, and you are his partner. He is not a woman and doesn't have a womb. Who else are we going to work with?"

"But . . ." I hesitated, still not convinced.

They spoke their next words sternly. "You have suffered, and you have transformed your pain into compassion and your sorrows into wisdom! Accept this call!"

How could I not? I was grateful for the guidance they'd offered me in the past, so I surrendered to what they were asking of me. I would show up as instructed.

Alberto had already been a witness to my healing journey and to my relationship with this lineage of midwives. Thus, when I told him about my experience in the jungle, he recognized that it was a great blessing. He gladly embraced the Rite of the Womb as part of the Munay-Ki.

A few months later, I had the opportunity to offer the Rite of the Womb to more than 600 women between New York, Miami, and California, within a Great Shamanic initiation guided by Alberto and by three Q'ero shamans, including Doña Juana Apaza, who accompanied me in offering the initiation. From there, the Rite of the Womb swiftly traveled around the world; today, thousands of women have shared the blessings in more than 60 countries.

THE CAULDRON OF TRANSFORMATION

This rite is focused on the energetic womb, the creative center, and it is transmitted from woman to woman. She, who is offering the rite, activates the wisdom of the lineage by placing both hands over her belly and saying, "The womb is not a place to store fear and pain, the womb is to create and give birth to life." Then, while leaving one hand on her belly, she reaches with the other hand over the womb of the woman receiving the transmission and repeats the same words.

When experienced as a stand-alone rite, it provides healing, helping to clear intense emotions, heaviness, or illness. Even if a woman lost her physical womb, she has the energetic matrix, meaning she can still receive and transmit the Rite of the Womb.

I have received hundreds of testimonials from women who received the blessing. One of the first letters came from a woman who was diagnosed with cancer and was ready to have a full hysterectomy. However, the day after she received the Rite of the Womb, she got her period (after seven months of no menstruation), which helped to expel the tumors. She said to me, "I am no longer in menopause, and I am cancer-free. My uterus is back to cleansing, and I am in my new path. I had the honor of offering my blood to Pachamama and burying it in the earth. My doctors have transferred me from oncology to specialized gynecology. They are still trying to understand what is no longer there."

The Rite of the Womb touches women in all kinds of different ways—some miraculous and some more subtle. As with the other rites of the Munay-Ki, if the wisdom of the lineage has been dormant, it is awakened; and if it is already awakened, it is empowered. The woman whose cancer was cured underwent an extraordinary healing, and I am sure that her own determination to change toxic patterns in her life was as much the catalyst for her miraculous recovery as the Rite of the Womb. She had begun paying attention to her womb and her experience of femininity, and the rite gave her the extra push she needed to heal.

Other examples of healing through the Rite of the Womb abound. Women who had painful periods found ease in their flow; others who suffered from irregular menstrual cycles found a comfortable rhythm; women who had experienced sexual abuse went deeper into their healing journey; and some who could not feel pleasure in their bodies connected with their sensuality. I also received news from women who had been longing to become pregnant for some time and did not conceive until their wombs were blessed by the lineage. In addition, I heard from women who found peace after the physically and emotionally unsettling experience of an abortion.

Many women experience a newfound sense of appreciation for their wombs and the life-giving capacity they hold—not only for the possibility of birthing a child but also as an energetic container for creativity and healing. Many discover their womb as an aspect of themselves they had once taken for granted or forgotten completely. They reconcile with their femininity, which includes learning to be comfortable with darkness and the unknown (which is also symbolic of the journey of pregnancy, as the fetus grows in the darkness of the womb) and to follow their natural cycles.

In every ceremony where I have offered this rite, I have witnessed tears—from deep grieving to profound joy. The Rite of the Womb can be deeply emotional for transgender people. Those who were once women are able to fully mourn what no longer is, or they may rejoice at this new way of honoring their uterus, even if they do not identify as female anymore. And those who were once men are excited about their initiation into a sisterhood and feel a greater sense of connection to their energetic womb. The sentiments are as unique as each of the people connecting with this lineage.

I have related the many ways in which the Rite of the Womb can have significant effects on an individual's life. However, it can also have ramifications on the level of the collective. We are in times of great change, and from a feminine perspective, we can refer to this as a moment of renewal during which the old must die to create space for the new to be born. It is natural to experience painful contractions as the old structures break apart so that life may compost that energy and offer nourishment to this new phase of humanity.

In many ways, we are in the pressure cooker, stripping away the past so that we can emerge into a pristine new destiny. That's an opportunity that is offered by the Rite of the Womb: to courageously descend into the womb of the Earth—much like the ancient Sumerian goddess Inanna, who was stripped of her possessions as she journeyed to the underworld so that she could emerge purified as the Queen of Heaven and Earth. This "underground" journey is the feminine aspect of the hero's journey. For she understands that the path she walks is not solely external; it is a process of deep incubation and deconstruction of her ego and her fears. This is how we make it through the "eye of the needle" that represents safe passage through the pachakuti. This is how we slough off our old skins, like a serpent, in order to birth a new destiny for ourselves and all our relations—the ones who crawl, fly, swim, and walk on two or many legs.

We have the opportunity to give birth to these new times and the world for which we yearn. However, we cannot expect to birth anything of great value if our center of creative power is full of fear and other dense energies. And given that hysterectomies, the partial or total removal of the uterus and reproductive organs, are one of the most common surgeries in the Western world today, it is clear that too many of us continue to harbor shame, pain, and the traumas of the past—including what we inherited from our mothers and grandmothers—within our powerful regenerative center or matrix: the place where we should be sowing the seeds of our yearnings and the destinies we want. For the legacy of the feminine is not only filled with the gifts of our fertility but also contains the traumas of yesterday.

THE GIFT OF BLOOD

For many women in the Western world, menarche (the first occurrence of menstruation) is not met with the celebratory rituals found in ancient cultures in which the rite of passage toward womanhood was viewed as a sacred gift. Indeed, the religious tradition in which Western culture is steeped has continually stressed the "sinfulness" of the female, even going so far as to term menstruation a "curse" that was brought upon Eve as a punishment for succumbing to temptation and eating the forbidden fruit from the Tree of Knowledge. This interpretation is likely a distortion of a much older story—one that celebrates the mysteries of the feminine that is symbolized by the red apple, the tree, the snake, and the garden, all of which stand as powerful symbols of fertility and primordial wisdom of the feminine.

Even women who were raised in a more egalitarian world are susceptible to the dangerous, distorted version of this myth, which casts half the world's population in the role of cursed, irrational, sinful temptress. A woman's body, with its feminine curves and menstrual cycle that spans the same amount of time as an entire moon cycle, is not particularly revered for its life-giving wonders, as it was in the ancient pagan cultures that prevailed before the dawn of Christianity. Because our ideas about sexuality, fertility, and the body are so deeply rooted in shame and silence, it is little wonder that Western women have allowed these false ideas. We may be utterly unconscious that we harbor these notions, but our wombs, which are energetic custodians of our emotions, are fully aware of such mindsets.

The Rite of the Womb has the capacity to clear out the negative attitudes toward the female body that may be covertly influencing us physically, emotionally, mentally, and spiritually. One of my senior students, Namasté, shares the beautiful evolution of her own relationship with her womanhood:

I got my period when I was 11 years old on a mountain trekking trip with a friend and her dad. Since we were hundreds of miles away from civilization and no adult that I trusted was around, I hid it for five days. I thought I was still a child, and I wanted to live like one: carefree—camping, swimming, climbing trees. Instead, I was going to have to deal with sanitary napkins, making sure I didn't stain my clothes with menstrual blood. I hated my womb for this betrayal: menstruation was disgusting and unfair.

As the years went by, there were times I couldn't afford sanitary napkins—my mom spent most of our money on booze and drugs—so I had to stay home until the bleeding was over. At 18, I started taking birth control pills, which changed my life. Now I had predictability, no more heavy bleeding and cramps, no more staining—and hell, I could even decide not to have my period. I stayed on the pill for 33 years. I never wanted children, so my period was useless, a burden—in fact, I considered everything about being a woman a burden.

By the time I received the Rite of the Womb in 2017, I had been thinking about getting off the pill for about a year. I had begun taking better physical care of myself—exercising regularly, eating healthier, sleeping longer—and consequently I'd begun wondering about the number of hormones and chemicals I was putting into my body through the pill.

When I heard the prayer, "The womb is not a place to store fear and pain, the womb is to create and give birth to life," it dawned on me. I had been storing all my crap in my womb! My womb had long been a repository for my fear of being a grown woman, all my pain for being a woman, all the suffering I associated with womanhood. And when I said the words as I was giving this rite to my fellow women, everything clicked into place for me: why I was there and what I needed to do next.

I quit the pill for good. For the next three months, I bled twice a month and nurtured the rite every time. I washed away decades of fear and pain that had been festering in my womb. By physically giving them back to Earth through my blood, I understood how they were transformed in love, compassion, and life. I also noticed I was becoming more creative, less self-conscious, and less ashamed of my body, my period, and womanhood. My menstrual blood was a cord from my core to the heart of the Earth, and the pulse of my blood was the pulse of the Earth, too. For the first time, I felt how I was Earth's daughter, and how her power lived within me. I felt stronger, lighter, calmer, wiser, more connected with the Divine and my own divine nature. I felt alive.

For a few years, my blood was the vessel to offer myself to Earth; now it is red wine, for I bleed only once or twice a year. The Rite of the Womb has become a simple yet powerful way to get acquainted with the eternal and sacred dance between birth, life, and death, over and over again. It's a simple and beautiful way of becoming a woman.

CLEARING THE VESSEL OF THE WOMB AND STEPPING INTO FEMININE POWER

The Rite of the Womb offers a purification ritual to help us realize that we have the power to release what holds us back so that we can give birth to the new times that await us over the horizon. It allows our power center, our womb, to incubate and birth our dream of a golden age to come.

However, just as the womb sheds its layers (the endometrium) every month, we must apply the same amount of rigor and intentionality to clearing out our disempowering beliefs and opening up to our true creative power, which is our birthright. In the years after the midwives revealed themselves to me, I came to understand that the stillbirth they had helped me deliver symbolized the death that women carry when we shut down our power as creators. This is not only an individual matter; it is a global occurrence that began more than 4,000 years ago when the Goddess was relegated to a subordinate position and overshadowed by an almighty masculine god.

The lineage of midwives is ancient, and it predates the ascendancy of the monotheistic god. The village and communities of the women who came to me in my vision were subjugated more than 2,000 years ago. Since then, they have existed in the ethereal realms and recently have returned to steward us back into a healthy relationship with the feminine.

The Rite of the Womb's lineage are women who were brave enough to free themselves from suffering. In my first vision, they shared with me, "We have come at this time to remind women that you are not here to suffer. Please remember that you are the creatrixes of the world you want for your children's children. Let's clean and clear your womb so you can recover the power to create what you yearn for."

Knowing that all humans come into the world through the womb, they want us to be aware that all life—whether this is a human life or some other creation—must be incubated in a loving space. The lineage of the Rite of the Womb wants us to remember that the womb is a place to create and give birth to life. Thus, the womb must be a pure vessel, as it carries the generations to come. And even for those who do not have physical wombs or who don't choose to birth children, the womb represents the creative potential of the sacral chakra, which is the birthplace of our personal dreams—so it's vital to keep it clear of toxic influences.

This initiation clears the womb so that it can be a pristine vessel for all that we choose to birth in our lives. It also teaches the initiate how to sow the seeds of the beauty they wish to create and works in tandem with all the other rituals. The initiate first harnesses their desire from the level of the Healer and Daykeeper, nurtures that desire with the discernment of the Wisdomkeeper, continues to grow it with the vision and love of the Earthkeeper, and ushers it into the world with the help of the Creator.

The Rite of the Womb helps us to remember that despite any suffering or trauma we may have experienced, we do not have to remain victims to the stories of our past. We have all been graced with the power of renewal; no matter how many figurative deaths we have been through, the grieving process always gives way to new life. Thus, the Rite of the Womb helps us to navigate the obstacles that stand in the way of our commitment to be the change we wish to see in the world. The rite helps us nurture our wombs, free of heavy emotions; otherwise, we may birth children and other creations that will experience a disproportionate sense of insecurity. We want whatever we create to be playful and have trust in the Universe. Think of a child who is incubated for nine months in a womb that is heavy with grief; when this occurs, the primordial makeup of their body will be laden with a sense of adversity and inadequacy right from the moment of conception.

As I began offering the Rite of the Womb, the process of reclaiming my power occurred naturally. I became more confident about my abilities as a teacher, and I came to understand that I was supported by a lineage who believed in my capacity to share the Rite of the Womb. For me, reclaiming power was not about turning into a different version of myself; it was about honestly and openly recognizing my unpolished gifts and expanding my willingness to offer them to others.

I should also say that for women who are on a journey to reclaim their power, the Rite of the Womb is not about "turning the tables" or excluding and dismissing men. Many men have lost a sense of connection to their deep personal power, and in order to achieve a sense of harmony on this planet, we must learn to work together and coax one another's true gifts to the surface. With the Rite of the Womb, the masculine and feminine are invited to come into balance. While women share the rite with one another, the men (and anyone who prefers this option) are asked to become stewards of the ceremony and hold sacred space for the women in their lives (wife, mother, sisters, daughters, or other). At the end of the ceremony, a blessing is bestowed upon the men.

The men and others who prefer this way can imagine themselves inside the womb—either their mother's womb or the archetypal womb in which all of us were incubated and dreamed into existence. Then, the women, standing in a circle around these people, offer the rite from their womb to this energetic mother womb. This blessing can clear negative imprints inherited from the time in utero, when we were not separate from our mothers and absorbed her emotions and other chemical information from her as well as her surroundings. It can also clear a negative relationship to the mother and to the feminine.

As we work with the Rite of the Womb and continue to clear our psyches and bodies of difficult energies that have been lodged in our most potent life center, we empower ourselves and others to make a difference. We can't expect someone else to take charge. As powerful women, we reclaim what was denied to us for so long, recognizing that we have the support of a lineage to help us in doing our share. We may experience this in our families, homes, neighborhoods, and communities. Eventually, everything we do we offer for the well-being of all the generations to come and for our planet.

As women who are opening our hearts, we learn to incubate healthy dreams for the world. We may envision our great-grandchildren thriving, and all children in the world going to bed with full, happy bellies—all children in the world living amid peace and love. We may also envision all women living in homes free of violence and scarcity.

It goes without saying that we are in times of great change. The world has been turned upside down, and we sit in the darkness— the void and womb of rebirth—waiting for what is to emerge. We stand at the precipice of an evolutionary opportunity: to either be swallowed by the nightmare of history and rocked back to sleep or to become cartographers of our own destiny, dreaming a new golden age into being. As we experience this collective dark night of the soul, the choice of where we go from here is ours.

Practice: Empower Your Womb

You can nurture the Rite of the Womb in the following ways. If you still menstruate, during your next cycle, find an intimate space to offer some of your menstrual blood to the earth. You may wish to bleed directly on the earth, or you can collect some of your blood in a small vial and pour it on the earth while repeating the following words:

I release my fear so I may embrace freedom.
I release my pain so I may embrace joy.
I release my anger so I may embrace compassion.
I release my sadness so I may embrace peace.
You can add any other words that ring true for you.

If you are in your years of plenitude (after menopause), then you can do a ritual on the next dark moon. Simply create an intimate space to offer red wine to the earth while repeating the words above and adding any other words that ring true for you.

If you are pregnant, you can offer flowers to Mother Earth during the full moon—and celebrate the life you carry in your womb. Repeat the following words:

I release my fear so I may embrace freedom.
I release my pain so I may embrace joy.
I release doubt so I may embrace truth.

Feel free to add any other words that ring true for you.

To empower your womb further, spend a full year (13 moon cycles) of ceremony, considering the above steps.

THE CONTINUATION

As we come to the end of this book, I am hesitant to call it a "conclusion" or an "epilogue," for in many ways, your journey, Dear Reader, has only just begun. The Munay-Ki Rites are transmissions that plant and nurture seeds of wisdom with the intention that they will flourish (perhaps even leading to the spread of new seeds!). My hope is that you will be inspired to discover even more insights within this wisdom tradition. Perhaps you will be motivated to take a class or workshop to formally receive the rites (please visit www.munay-ki.org to learn how and where to receive the rites), or maybe you will continue to work with the practices and questions within this book, which can lead to a lifetime of deep inquiry and wisdom. The more we engage with these practices on all levels of our lives—physical, emotional, mental, and spiritual—the more fruit these seeds will bear.

There are thousands of Munay-Ki practitioners around the world who can offer you the rites. You may find a practitioner in your area by visiting the directory within the munay-ki.org website. Also, you can find online and residential classes to receive the rites and to become a practitioner who can offer the rites to others. There are plenty of options in different languages.

The Munay-Ki is the wisdom of what we, as a human collective, are being asked to birth on this planet. We already know the consequences of life in a culture that devalues Earth and is based on domination and extraction rather than cooperation and the cultivation of beauty and hope. This has not worked for us, and we are ready for a new story.

The Munay-Ki Rites help us to become humbler about our nature as infinite beings inhabiting a temporary earthly form. We are made of bones, tissues, and minerals; each of us has a body, with nails and teeth and hair that fall out as we grow older. We are all vulnerable in these bodies, which become frail and deteriorate as we age. But even as the body decays, we have an opportunity to access the deeper knowledge of who we are and how we belong to Mother Earth and the Great Spirit. Even as we come closer to the threshold that leads to the realm beyond the flesh, we have the choice to become wiser and more compassionate—to wake up to our infinite natures and inspire all around us to do the same.

The Munay-Ki teachings are rooted in our humanity—in our experience as bodies that need to be fed with actual food and water and as beings who need to care for children, work and pay bills, and do all the things that are important to sustain our earthly incarnation. At the same time, these teachings allow us to connect to that infinite self that never perishes and continues to voyage through eons and eras. In understanding the full spectrum of our being, we can dare to realize our true self in the most holistic way.

To embody the values and spirit of the Munay-Ki, we must strive to be as present as we can. It may be tempting to tune out the anguish of the world, to feel overwhelmed by what the times are asking of us. The Munay-Ki, with each successive rite, gives us the tools to be here now and to have the strength and tenacity that emerge when we are rooted in something greater than us.

When we embody the healer, "here" is the physical body—with all its emotions and sensations, health and disease, light and shadow, wounds and gifts. "Now" is this very moment, right now, and the ability to respond to our immediate needs.

When we claim our Bands of Power, "here" is our connection with the elements, which exist both within and outside us. "Now" is immediate and accessible, but also eternal, as the elements are the building blocks of nature that have existed since the dawn of time on planet Earth.

With the Harmony Rite, we find "here" in our relationship with the archetypes that bridge our connection with our instinctual self and with our being beyond ordinary reality. "Now" becomes a multidimensional dance of allowing our bodies to respond to whatever is before us with our full wisdom and capacity.

As we hone our capacity as a Seer, "here" is the complex eco-system of the world within and around us, with both its obvious and hidden charms and dangers. "Now" is not only the present but also our past conditioning and how it has come to shape our perceptions and interpretations of the moment—as well as our determination of how we wish to change.

For the Daykeeper, "here" is the community: the communal kitchen, the park, the places of gathering. It is also nature and the connection to the feminine—to the soft lap of Mother Earth and the land where we live, which sustains us. Because the Daykeeper welcomes the day, the night, and the seasons, "now" is the entirety of these cycles.

For the Wisdomkeeper, "here" is the summit of the mountain that overlooks not just one's own community but expands into the entire region as far as one can see. "Now" is one's entire life-time, which also allows for the contemplation of others' lifetimes.

The Earthkeeper is "here" on our beautiful planet, encompassing the oceans, volcanoes, land, and clouds. "Now" is not a single lifetime but the span of many generations, much like the Haudenosaunee philosophy—from the six Native American nations known as the Iroquois Confederacy—of making decisions today that will benefit seven generations into the future and honor seven generations into the past.

For the Starkeeper, "here" expands into the solar system, where they stand and contemplate the galaxy. Although they are located on Earth, they can sense the movement and orbits of all the moons and planets. "Now" inhabits much longer cycles, such as the thousand-year eras that ancient civilizations acknowledged. It offers the gift of prophecy, which helps us to intuitively know future possibilities, and it also includes the wisdom downloaded from galactic realms, such as the Pleiades constellation, or from interdimensional beings who are able to communicate with the most receptive among us.

For the Creator, "here" is the entire Universe, centered on the sun. For among the ancient people of the Andes, it was crucial to be luminous like the sun—to develop the light within us that lives hidden in the fertile darkness. "Now" is the birth and expansion of the Universe, so it is infinite and ultimately timeless.

For the Rite of the Womb, "here" is in the womb, where the Great Divine Mother joins with the Earth Mother to shed death and cultivate life and creativity. And "now" is in the moon cycles that create the rhythmic ebb and flow of the waters and emotions, making the human life a richer experience.

May you continue to nurture the seeds of the rites within you and be the embodiment of the hope that we require on our planet today. Ultimately, this book is a gift of hope, from my heart to yours. I am not speaking of hope as an ethereal concept, but as a full-bodied reality that is rooted in love and our capacity to be creators of our individual and collective destinies.

My wish is that you will discover and express your fullness and originality—that you will embrace all that you are, including the limitations that are intrinsic to our humanity. Our physical and emotional limitations offer the opportunity to test the greatness of our souls, our love, our spirits, our visions, and everything about us that lives well beyond this human body. In truth, the physical container is not a hindrance; it is a creative limitation that gives us enough of a pressure cooker to encourage us not to live a complacent life.

We have been given gifts, energies, and resources, and we must not squander them by assuming that they will be here forever. Instead, we can appreciate and use them wisely to help others. *Ultimately, the path of the Munay-Ki is about service.* This is how our munay (love) keeps growing—and so does our abundance. The more we give, the more that comes our way. Of course, the minute we shift our motivation to giving because we only want to receive something else, we are not in ayni *or* sacred reciprocity.

Living in connection with the sacred at all times, however, is not merely about our ideas of what is needed or about the actions we take. It is also about surrendering to the great mystery of existence. In the mystical traditions of the Andes, there are things that can be known but not told—that which cannot be explained but that can be directly experienced. But beyond these experiences, there is the deep mystery so infinite that it may never be known. From a shamanic perspective, it is not about understanding with a logical mind how it all works, but about the willingness to surrender so deeply as to merge with the Great Mystery's precious gems. This is like a divine touch that infuses us with inspiration and creativity and greater compassion and a sense of what others might need. The Munay-Ki Rites help us to continually commit to keeping our hearts open so that we can experience reality in a more naked, essential way—and so we can see things as they are in order to recognize where our own efforts will be most effective.

The Munay-Ki Rites also help us become more comfortable with stillness. This is a difficult endeavor in a world that is accustomed to moving at warp speed. Some of the most powerful changes that we can make require slowness and contemplation. For example, instead of getting caught up in the speed and drama of our daily lives, making us feel the need to take a vacation to "reset," we can turn the environment around us into a sanctuary so that we no longer feel the need to escape our lives. Rather, we ourselves can become the oasis of peace, beauty, and harmony that we long for. This is a sacred form of activism.

Once we have experienced the kind of transformation that allows us to embrace the unobstructed goodness that is at the core of who we are, we can act on our pure munay. We can change the world. And we can become stewards of a better tomorrow.

APPENDIX

The wisdom of the Munay-Ki is meant to connect you with your own essence, love, and potential. The insight and medicine of the lineages will guide you in the areas of your life where you need clarity and growth. As you integrate these transmissions, you feel ever more rooted in the gift of your human life and ever more liberated into the boundless infinity of your being. The Munay-Ki is a path to realizing your freedom while creating a life in loving relationship with all nature and a just relationship with all peoples.

THE PI STONE—A SYMBOL OF THE MUNAY-KI

A traditional altar of the Andean shaman is a *mesa* or *misha*—a bundle of sacred stones and objects. On the Munay-Ki path, practitioners are encouraged to anchor their connection to the medicine on one stone: the Pi stone. These stones date back to before the Inka Empire and symbolize a gateway from the material realm to a more subtle dimension. The shape of the stone, known as a torus, symbolizes the journey of the sun across the sky, while the hole in the center captures the void-essence of the energetic universe and our inherent oneness. Pi stones are keys to the stars and powerful instruments for healing, as they serve to transmit energy from the invisible to the manifest world, and vice versa. The stone also represents the continuity of life and death and the capacity for transformation and renewal. I advise anyone who wishes to work with the Munay-Ki Rites to keep a Pi stone on their altar to remind them of their communion with this lineage—it is similar to taking refuge in their timeless wisdom and making a sacred contract with them.

It serves as an amulet and a reminder that we never walk alone (you can also wear it as a necklace). There is tremendous help available to us if we know how to align ourselves with it.

CREATING YOUR MUNAY-KI ALTAR

An altar is a metaphor for your connection to the Great Spirit. It is the space where you can bring your healing intentions to life and where you can consciously communicate with spiritual allies. If you are feeling scattered or unbalanced, you can turn to your altar—perhaps light a candle, burn incense or palo santo, and reassemble the objects—to feel more centered and clarify your intentions.

You can empower the process of cultivating a connection with the Munay-Ki Rites and their corresponding lineages by creating an altar with the symbols and qualities you wish to bring into ceremony. First, find a physical space where you can hold your sacred objects indefinitely (until you decide that it is time to transform that space into something else). You can always start somewhere and then move if necessary. Next, dedicate a flat surface for this purpose—it can be a table, a raw piece of wood, or even the floor—and cover it with a cloth that feels special to you.

Then, follow the guidelines below as you make progress with each rite.

The Healer Rite

Find a Pi stone (you can find them online) and sit with it in front of your altar. Connect to your deep desire to walk the path of the healer, and then blow your commitment into your stone, anchoring your intentions. As you summon the lineage of healers from the Andes and from around the world, place your Pi stone over the cloth and light a candle to offer your own light to the lineage and to those who need healing. In this way you are already participating in the great wave of healing that is traveling over the world. Congratulations! You can sit daily in front of your altar to keep renewing your healer vows. Each time you do, offer a candle and perhaps some kind of incense to all those who seek warmth, light, and healing.

The Bands of Power Rite

The Bands of Power invite us to cultivate a more conscious and sacred relationship with the elements—earth, water, fire, air, and pure light. Collect some earth (it can be from a special place) in a small bowl and place it near the south direction of your altar. Next, pour some water (it can also be from a special place) in a small bowl or inside a shell and place it near the west direction of your altar. Then find a beautiful candle (hopefully made with nontoxic wax) and place it near the north side of your altar. For the east direction find some feathers that can represent the air element.

Once the four elements are set, light the candle to activate the energy of your altar, then spend time in quiet contemplation until you feel your mind and heart relaxing. Take a few deep breaths to relax even further and invite pure light to shine on your life's path. You can also burn incense as an offering to everyone and everything that you included in your altar.

The Harmony Rite

To honor our allies from the Harmony Rite, we place a representation of each one of them on the altar. We add the serpent in the south, jaguar in the west, hummingbird in the north, and eagle/condor in the east. In this way each of the elements will be very close to one of the archetypes: earth will be next to the serpent, water to the jaguar, fire to the hummingbird, and air to the eagle/condor. Then we figure out a representation for each of the three Guardians of the Lower, Middle, and Upper worlds. These three allies can be placed intuitively wherever it feels best.

Most often we find the representations of the different arche-types at different moments—days, weeks, or even months apart. Don't worry about this. Add the image or the object for an arche-type whenever you manage to find it, or as we say in shamanic lore, *whenever it finds you*. Once you have set the intention to work with the archetypes on your altar, pay attention, because it will show up sometimes in the least expected situations.

At any stage—with one, a few, or all the symbols for the arche-types placed on your altar—light the candle, offer incense, and meditate on their gifts and messages. You may even ask a specific question and contemplate the answer.

With the presence of your allies, your altar is becoming more and more empowered, helping you to access your own wisdom, love, and power.

The Seer Rite

As mentioned earlier, the children's book author Antoine de Saint-Exupéry famously said, "It is only with the heart that one can see rightly; what is essential is invisible to the eye." The Seer Rite is all about learning to see through the eyes of the heart. For this transmission, add an object to your altar that represents compassionate, loving, intuitive discernment. This object can be a heart-shaped stone or some other representation of the heart. At the same time, add a symbol of clear seeing with your spiritual eye. This can be a crystal or another gem that has transparency. In any case, look for elements that make you feel a tangible connection to the Seer Rite.

The Daykeeper Rite

In Mexico and other cultures with traditions rooted in pre-Columbian art, you'll find beautiful candleholders of multiple figures holding hands and embracing one another in a circle. This represents the community, and the light that is ignited in the center is for everyone's benefit—a great metaphor for the Daykeeper's lineage.

For this rite, place something on your altar, such as this pre-Columbian figurine of the circular candleholder, that demonstrates your commitment to building a positive connection and relationship with your chosen community. Also, be sure to add flowers, incense, and other forms of beauty to your physical altar—as all these things symbolize the sense of renewal and vitality that you are infusing into your wishes for your community.

The Wisdomkeeper Rite

For this rite, you are going to find a representation of a mountain to place on your altar. This may be a drawing, photo, or sculpture—or perhaps it is a container of soil or a small rock that comes from your favorite mountain. While looking for the representation, remember that it is not only about the physical body of the mountain but also its apu or tutelary spirit who will act as your guide and protector and who will steward you toward greater courage and awareness of your purpose, as well as your ability and love to live out this purpose.

After placing a symbol of your mountain on your altar, light a candle and make an offering of incense, palo santo, or anything else that rings true for you. Also, dedicate a prayer to your apu and allow a few moments of silence to receive its wisdom.

The Earthkeeper Rite

Now it's time to add an item to your altar that represents Mother Earth, Gaia, Pachamama. This may be an image or sculpture of our beautiful planet or an illustration of Mother Earth as a primeval goddess (the figure of Te Fiti, the goddess with the power to create life, from the Disney film *Moana* comes to mind). Just as the Gaia hypothesis helped us understand our home planet as a complex, living, breathing, conscious organism, the placement of Pachamama on our altar helps us cultivate a vast and global awareness that allows us to acknowledge the consciousness of our planet and to cultivate ayni with Mother Earth. Make sure to light at least one candle in her honor and make fragrant offerings of incense or other herbs.

The Starkeeper Rite

To remain connected with this lineage and embody its wisdom, find an image of a star or a constellation and place it on your altar. This can be a photo or a painting of the night sky; it could also be a meteorite—known in the Andes as "star travelers" and revered for their power. As you place this image or meteorite on your altar, imagine how the light from that distant sun had to travel for millions of miles to reach Earth or how that meteorite journeyed for decades from the edge of our solar system to land on our planet. Set your intention for it to always remind you of your place in the heavens and that you are a star traveler as well.

The Creator Rite

After contemplating what you long to create for yourself or for the world, find an item that can be a symbol of that. You can anchor your desired creation by using your breath—softly exhale through the mouth onto the object—while visualizing an image and any feelings you have about it. Then place that object on your altar.

You can repeat this process with the creations that you have already manifested and want to nurture or the things—the people or events—that you want to release. Find the object or symbol, blow into it the energy that you want to anchor to it, and then place it on the altar.

In this way, your manifesting (as a co-creator of your life and destiny as well as your surroundings) is safeguarded in the sacred space of the Munay-Ki, and you can count on all the lineages and allies of this path to be your guides and helpers.

Remember to light a candle and make your offerings as you approach your altar and awaken the energies held by its symbols.

The Rite of the Womb

For this initiation, you can contemplate what it means for you to be free of suffering (still accepting that pain is part of life and is not the same as suffering). Once you tap into a feeling or idea of this, then you can anchor it with a gentle exhale on your object of choice. Before placing it on your altar, take a moment to connect with this lineage of women who remind us that we are powerful creatresses, and blow your prayers to them on that same object. Then place your piece on the altar and light a candle, followed by offerings of incense, flowers, or anything else you like.

GRATITUDES

The Munay-Ki exists only because of Alberto Villoldo's courage and dedication to share the rites with his students and the world beyond. My heart beats in expansive gratitude for him and his mentor Don Manuel Quispe from the Q'ero people, as well as the wisdomkeepers who preceded them.

I am also deeply indebted to all the paqos from the Q'ero nation who continue to share the rites with our students when we are in Peru and abroad. Special thanks to Humberto Soncco, Pascual Apaza, Francisco Chura, Juanita Apaza, Juan Apaza, Pablo Cruz, Juan Quispe, the late Mariano Apaza, and Bernardina Apaza. Hailing from other Andean villages are Porfirio Sequeiros and Martin Piñedo.

My ongoing appreciation extends to all teachers of the Four Winds Society who have cultivated the medicine of the rites, and who over the years have transmitted them with impeccability and passion. I am especially grateful to Karen Hoza, Maria Clara Castañeda, Antonella Velásquez, Steffen Büffel, Sebastián Hidalgo, Laura Heart, Fernanda Gómez, Martha Abbott, Karen Johnson, Elise Kost, Martina Seiner, Namaste Reategui, Bernhard Luscher, Thomas Kleiner, Folan Lay, and Jill Devi Shri.

I give thanks to Hay House vice-president and publisher Patty Gift for believing in the wisdom and message of *The Sacred Andean Codes*; and to my editors Nicolette Salamanca and Lara Asher for their kind and talented guidance. Further, I acknowledge Hay House's president and CEO, Reid Tracy, and the entire team for their unwavering support.

At the beginning of this project, Olivia Weil helped me compile the Munay-Ki teachings I shared with students. Then, writer Jennifer

Gandin Le continued gathering material that Alberto and I had written or recorded. In the end, Nirmala Nataraj offered additional grace and insight to my writing. I am grateful to all three!

I also want to thank my fabulous, international team of collaborators at the Four Winds Society: Pablo Sütterlin, Thomas Schwarz, Benjamin Ulrich, Verena Ledig, Barbora Hanova, Andrea Fernández, Tracey Chandler, Isabel Elia, Samanta Giordani, Deborah Stucchi, José Tomás Fuentes, and Torsten Buder.

Much love and gratitude goes to my family and friends who constantly encourage my mystical endeavors. Special thanks to my mother, Victoria Frias; to my sons, Kelly Miles and Meric Abel; to my stepdaughter, Alexis McCulloch; to my nephew, Tomás González; to my sister, Carolina González; and to my friends Monika Nataraj, Collette Baron-Reid, and Francisca Olalquiaga.

To my students and fellow seekers, thank you for walking this path with me. Your questions, perspectives, and openness have enriched my own understanding of the Munay-Ki and deepened my commitment to sharing these teachings with others. Special appreciation to Katrin Schultze, Jillian Vogtli, and Anna Xrisanthopoulou for your powerful testimonies.

Lastly, I am deeply grateful to you, the reader, for your curiosity and willingness to embark on this journey of self-discovery and transformation. It is my sincere hope that *The Sacred Andean Codes* serves as a source of inspiration, healing, and empowerment in your life.

ABOUT THE AUTHOR

Marcela Lobos has been initiated in the healing and spiritual traditions of the Amazon and the Andes. She is the author of the book *Awakening Your Inner Shaman* and the co-author of *Mystical Shaman Oracle cards*. Born and raised in Chile, Marcela graduated from a prestigious journalism program. Later she pursued studies in yoga and wellness and completed the Healing the Light Body School of the Four Winds Society in 2005. Today she is a teacher at the same school and spearheads its Spanish wing. Throughout the last decade, Marcela has led hundreds of students through the Medicine Wheel and Munay-Ki programs. She also travels internationally to lead sacred journeys for women to awaken their own power, grace, and wisdom. She lives between Chile and the United States with her husband, Alberto Villoldo. Visit her work online at www.marcelalobos.com or www.munay-ki.org.

CONNECT WITH

HAY HOUSE

ONLINE

🌐 hayhouse.co.uk   **f** @hayhouse

📷 @hayhouseuk   🐦 @hayhouseuk

▶ @hayhouseuk   ♪ @hayhouseuk

Find out all about our latest books & card decks • Be the first to know about exclusive discounts • Interact with our authors in live broadcasts • Celebrate the cycle of the seasons with us • Watch free videos from your favourite authors • Connect with like-minded souls

'The gateways to wisdom and knowledge are always open.'

Louise Hay